Endorsements

"At a time when we all are forced to introspect and make changes in how we perceive life and what we want from it, this book seems like an ideal guide. It gives you clarity in thoughts and helps you pave a path that aligns with your dreams, conscious, and heart."

Divya Kaushik
Special Correspondent, *Delhi Times*

"Beautifully woven [book] to enlighten, inspire, and transform you."

Ravi Garg
Director, WhatsApp India

"What sets it apart from the contemporary books penned by the New Age motivational gurus is its simplistic treatment, explaining the art and science of the most vital force—thought-power, with easy-to-do self-help tools."

Shekhar Srivastava
Ex-Group General Manager, ONGC

"A bible on how to accomplish happiness, peace, and prosperity. A must-read during these times."

Neeti Nigam
Assistant Editor, Indianexpress.com

. . . *continued*

"This book puts a structure and brings in an understanding of how our mind works with a perfect blend of roles being played by different aspects such as psychology, our ancient history, science, and so on. It further builds on crystalising how the above-mentioned aspects take either of the extreme circumstances we deal with in life and how we can move mountains only if we know how to navigate to the positive side of extremes and make a way out. The author has done commendable work in putting it all together and explaining to the reader not only 'Why' but equally 'How' one can learn to change the course and come out victorious."

Toshi Kaushik
Nation Talent Leader, Risk Advisory, Deloitte India

"In this trendsetting book, Swati Srivastava puts across actionable, practical steps based on scientific research to live a happy and fulfilling life. If you could only read one book this year, you have it in your hands."

Lt. Col. Pradeep Khare
Author, Columnist, TEDx Speaker, and Award-Winning YouTuber

"*The Magnetic Power of Your Thoughts* is a good book for the students of teacher education programme and for teachers who have a keen interest in shaping the future generations of the nation."

Dr Munesh Kumar
Director, School of Teacher Education, and Dean, Faculty of Education, CSJM University

THE MAGNETIC POWER OF YOUR THOUGHTS

A Guidebook for Creating a Happy and Abundant Life

SWATI SRIVASTAVA

HAY HOUSE

Hay House Publishers India

Australia • India
United Kingdom • United States

Hay House Publishers (India) Pvt. Ltd.
Muskaan Complex, Plot No.3, B-2 Vasant Kunj, New Delhi-110 070, India
Hay House Inc., PO Box 5100, Carlsbad, CA 92018-5100, USA
Hay House UK, Ltd., The Sixth Floor, Watson House, 54 Baker Street, W1U 7BU, UK
Hay House Australia Pty Ltd., 18/36 Ralph St., Alexandria NSW 2015, Australia

Email: contact@hayhouse.co.in
www.hayhouse.co.in

Reprint 2023

ISBN 978-93-91067-85-4
ISBN 978-93-91067-93-9 (e-book)

Printed at Repro India Limited

Dedicated to my grandmother, Late Krishna Srivastava,
whose love and warmth will stay with me forever.

"Oh, weary heart, laden with earth's weight and care,
Oh, feet, stumbling on the way, bleeding and bare,
Oh, arms outstretched, and hands upheld in prayer,
Oh, back, which so oft has felt the lash and rod,
Oh, soul, which cries aloud for the living God,
Oh, life, struggling to free itself from the clod;
Know this: there is no power from without,
Yourself must answer every fear and meet all doubt
With some divine, indwelling power
Which you yourself, upon yourself, shall shower;
And giving, take, and taking, give
Unto that life which you, yourself, shall live."

—*The Science of Mind* by Ernest Holmes

Contents

Introduction

"Do not wait for something outside of you to change something inside of you."
—Dr Joe Dispenza (author)

Do you want to live a life of excellence? Do you want to make a dent in the universe? Do you want to earn prosperity by walking on the path of your passion? Do you want to bathe in good health every day? Or, do you want to live a mediocre life, where you are meant to pay your bills and return home exhausted to an infuriating family? If you ever thought about reshaping your life, reaching for the pinnacles, and accomplishing your goals then you are at the right place.

Nowadays, mostly everyone is craving for some or the other material object to make their life merrier. If you are not one of those, then maybe you are searching for contentment in your relationships, in your jobs, or even in your social media posts. You are unaware of the fact that to make life merrier and worth living for, you need to reflect within rather than depend on some external object or person. You are unaware of the fact that you are a wholesome human being, complete in each and every aspect. The feeling of fulfilment you are striving for can be achieved by you alone. No other materialistic or unmaterialistic relationship can offer you what you can offer to yourself. The journey of living each moment in bliss starts within. You can only become a person of your dreams by identifying and working upon what you are capable of. Nothing can ever change this fundamental truth. The power to be your best lies within you which can unlock the miracle-life you dream about living. And this book is about reminding you of your forgotten power.

Some people acquire great abundance and happiness in a short time and with easy efforts; some require a long time and a lot more efforts, while some others are not able to acquire it at all and keep struggling throughout their life. Why do you think this happens? If this was due to inherited wealth, physical strength, or exceptional IQ, then every person possessing any one of the above qualities would remain prosperous throughout their life. But this is not the case and thus there must be something else which needs to be explored.

Those who can achieve the goals in their bucket list are harnessing the power of their thoughts in the right direction, consciously or unconsciously. This power has many names, but I will call it 'thought-power', as this term explains it the best. Each moment of your life, the thoughts you radiate out from your mind are creating and shaping your day. Anyone who can proactively apply thought-power in their life can acquire whatsoever they desire without the effect of the present or past conditions. If you firmly believe in your dreams, then there is no one who can stop you from living the life you desire. You can have the life partner you want, your dream house, good food on your plate, perfect health, academic excellence, a successful business, a reputed job, a fulfilled life . . . basically, anything you want.

If you have come across this book, then believe me that it is a sign that you have attracted a guidebook on living purposefully and joyfully. Through this book, life has given you a chance to change the way you have been living. It will help you regain the lost connection with the most important person in the world—'I'. It is going to teach you the what, why, and how of thought-power. It compiles and introduces some of the best ways of harnessing the extraordinary potential carried by each human being. It will help you in understanding how you can work the surrounding energy of the universe in your favour. You will also come to know how uncomplicated it is to achieve your goals.

Now, the question arises that why is this astounding concept not a topic of household discussion, and why is it not practised and taught by our education system? The reason is that the present human race has lost this knowledge as generations passed by. Also, the very fact of the extraordinary potential of human beings may have made it a formidable or daunting concept to be popularised. The knowledge of thought-power has remained confined to certain traditions, groups, and practitioners who still live by it, each day.

Today, a part of the scientific community has started to accept this power of free will, which the ancient cultures of the East and West have always known. Studies and ample amount of research in cosmology, quantum physics, neuroscience, psychology, epigenetics, parapsychology, history, etc., point towards an unfathomable power of the human mind and the energy field of the universe. This omnipresent energy field around us—which science, religion, and people have given different names such as higher intelligence, inner guide, source, etc.—is the basis of the entire existence. Tapping into this energy field with coherent and focused thoughts helps in acquiring all that one wishes to enjoy in life.

This book is about much more than positive thinking. It considers a wider and deeper topic of how our brain, mind, and energy of the universe are entangled in a huge web where the dance of creation takes place. It considers the overall aspect of why and how a proactive use of thought-power will work sometimes and why it may fail other times!

The book does not promote unreasonable or fairy-tale ideas. Do not be a blind acceptor of the facts shared here. Try it for yourself and then consider acknowledging them. But the ultimate point to remember is that whether you remain a firm believer or a sceptic, thought-power will always work!

If you have some previous knowledge of thought-power but have been too sceptic to believe in it due to your own know-how or from the peer or societal pressure, then just ask yourself, "Has this sceptical attitude helped me till now?" I do not think your answer will be an emphatic, "Yes!", else you would not have been holding this book in your hand. Without full participation from your side, any spiritual or scientific theory will be worthless. Do not discard the facts shared here as some New Age mumbo jumbo. After all, your present and future depend on it. If a read of some 200 pages can take your life to some unique level then isn't it worth trying? And once you have finished reading this book, there will be no stones left unturned when it comes to the knowledge of thought-power.

I have come up with this idea of writing a book, covering all the aspects of thought-power because there remains a gap in its popularity and successful application even after it has become a much-written-upon topic these days. Superficial knowledge of positive thinking and thought-power is insufficient to reap its full benefits. Thereby, the book aims at bridging the gap between the knowledge and application of thought-power. It tries to connect the infinite power of energy with the unfathomable power of our mind in order to create our desired reality. It is packed with just enough science, super-motivating facts, ample examples, and a foolproof action plan.

There are four different levels for efficient application of thought-power, and when the individual has taken care of all these levels, only then the desired result can be created. These levels are as follows:

- **Level 1 - Awareness of thought-power:**

  Chapter 1 will introduce you to the power of your thoughts and the benefits of positive thinking.

- **Level 2 - Dealing with scepticism:**

  Chapter 2 tries to clear your prejudices and scepticism regarding thought-power. Until you fully believe in this potential, you will never be able to have enough faith to utilise it to the maximum. After some focus on the history of thought-power, I talk about why science has started saying yes to thought-power. Few of the many mind-boggling scientific experiments have been shared which will leave you in awe and shoot up your faith in your abilities. It does not matter whether you understand the underlying scientific principle behind the working of thought-power. What matters is that you believe in this power which you hold within yourself.

- **Level 3 - Role of the subconscious mind:**

  Without considering thought-power and the subconscious mind side by side, you can never gain complete benefits of this power. In real life, only a healthy mind can lead to healthy thoughts and a bright future. Chapter 3 deals with the reconditioning of your subconscious mind for more empowering beliefs that will make you unstoppable.

- **Level 4 - Creating your reality with thought-power:** Once you become a firm believer of your inner power and have fuelled yourself with positive beliefs, this section gears you up for unidirectional and proactive thinking. How to have focused thoughts which are unstoppable is what you will learn here. The practise habits listed through Chapter 4 to 7 will help you manifest your desired reality.

If you are new to the concept of thought-power, this book will guide you through the basics and the ways of applying this wonderful concept. If you already know about thought-power but have been practising it without much success, you will come to know your shortcomings and the ways to change your approach. Your role as a reader should be to catch hold of inspiring details and examples and then make it stay with you for now and always.

Today, as you decide to read this book, it is not just a life-changing decision for you but also a delightful achievement for me as I get an opportunity to share this concept with you and make this world a better place to live in.

The journey to having a blissful state of affairs is not transcendental; it rather comes from within. If you can make a change within, then you have evolved as a human being capable of self-actualisation. So, get ready for a wonderful ride! When every ounce of energy within you will start saying yes to a beautiful life, miracles will happen and no doubts and fear will hinder your progress anymore. You will be a creator, a doer, a true being.

Let's begin together . . .

Chapter 1
The Limitless Potential of Your Thoughts

"Thought is a force—a manifestation of energy—having a magnet-like power of attraction."

—William Walker Atkinson (author)

Nature is a multitude of invisible and powerful forces, and their manifestations from time to time determine our survival or destruction. These intangible forces have always ruled the universe. Being a part of nature, you also have an invisible force, thought-power, residing within you. This force can either be a creator or a destroyer of your life. Once you understand this fact, you will be on your way to a more fulfilling life.

The Oxford dictionary defines thought as "An idea or opinion produced by thinking or occurring suddenly in the mind." Thoughts take birth in your mind. Your thoughts represent how you perceive the world. They are your outlook of the self and the surroundings. They depict your emotional status and your ways of comprehending and reacting to situations.

You Are the Creator of Your Destiny

You may have often come across the statement like "Thoughts become things", but rarely do you realise their underlying depth. Thoughts govern your reality. Whatever you are at present is because of the thoughts you had in your mind. Your thoughts are the ones to decide 'I can' or 'I cannot.' You have the same potential as anyone else, including those who accomplished what you wish for. The only difference is that they utilised their thought-power, consciously or unconsciously.

Your thought-power acts like a magnet that attracts corresponding things and situations towards you. Whatever you think predominantly in your mind will be attracted to you. If you place your thoughts in harmony with your desire, you will definitely get it. You can choose whatever you want in your life by visualising it in your mind. You can fulfil your dreams and achieve your goals by thinking about them in a dedicated manner. This happens without any doubts or exceptions. It's true that thoughts are magnetic, influential, and powerful tool beyond our imagination.

In this puppet stage show called life, your mind is the puppet master hiding behind the veils and holding the strings. The strings are your thoughts and the puppets are everything surrounding you—the people, situations, environment, etc. By moving the strings in different ways, the master can control the puppets. The best part is that the power always lies with the master; he can choose which puppet should enter the stage and which ones should leave. This analogy makes it clear that you are truly 'the master of your fate, the captain of your soul.' To change your life, start with changing your thoughts, as the people and conditions in it are because of your thoughts. No one has brought them up for you, except you.

Why do you have friends who share your character? Why do you fall for somebody who is just like one of your close friends or a family member? Why do you keep bumping into the same kind of fraudulent investors? All this is because you have attracted them into your life through your thought-power. Have you ever come across situations like getting a good news out-of-the-blue, accidentally bumping into a new client in an ATM queue, or receiving a call from a friend you were just thinking about in the morning? We often give them the name of magic, serendipity, coincidence, fate, déjà vu, luck, meant-to-be, etc. But in reality, these are all examples of your thought-power in action.

Throughout the day, you keep sending thoughts of varying intensities into the universe. At any point in time, by looking at the life you are living, your most influential thoughts can be predicted. Take a look around you, and you will know what has been cooking in your mind all the time. All occurrences in your life have resulted because you have given birth to them in your mind in the form of your thoughts. The quality of your life is always directly proportional to the quality of your thoughts. Your life is a reflection of your thoughts, so choose them carefully and evaluate their pros and cons. Then let them go out into the universe to come back to you in the form of your reality.

Your thoughts provoke you to act, and all actions you undertake lead to a reaction. Your every move will generate a consequence depending upon what it was. This is a cause-effect relationship that exists in our universe. Your thoughts are never ineffective, but you may not receive the desired outcome because you have not combined them properly with belief, emotions, and actions.

In terms of magic, this seems to be some kind of a superhuman power. But it's not. You need not be a superhero or an occult master to live a magnificent life. You just need to have specific thoughts that can bear fruit in real life. For some of you, it may seem hard to grasp that you attract everything into your life. Obviously, you are not a magician who can just lift the veil and a beautiful girl will appear out of thin air! But, my dear friend, what if I tell you that, in fact, you are the magician of your life. The way a magician makes use of optical illusions, you make use of thought energy to lead the life you have today.

Like a universal law, the thought-power is unbiased. It is continuously bringing to each one of you exactly those things that you have created in your mind. For the thought-power, you are equal; it does not check whether you are rich or poor, good or bad, young or old, or educated or uneducated. Your place of residence and your religious sentiments do not matter. Whether you believe in it or not and whether you understand it or not, does not matter. Your thought-power is impartial towards who you are but it guides your life every step of the way. It will always work whether you want it or not. It always has and it always will.

I hope it's a relief for all those who have been struggling with life to know that to accomplish their dreams and goals, the change needs to come from within and that the control does not lie with some outside hands. Things do not control you; you control things. With your crystal-clear intentions, you can draw towards you whatever you wish for.

Like the childhood rhyme, "Early to bed and early to rise makes a man healthy, wealthy, and wise," the conscious use of thought-power will make you healthy, wealthy, wise, and yes, happy too! Realise and appreciate the fact that your ability to think is your ability to change your life.

But why are thoughts so powerful? How do they determine your present and future? Your prolonged thoughts—the one uppermost in your mind most of the time—become the centre of creation and the energy of the universe around you conspires to convert it into reality. A scientific explanation of this is provided in Chapter 2.

Positive Mindset: A Road towards Happiness

"Our brains become magnetized with the dominating thoughts which we hold in our minds, and, by means with which no man is familiar, these 'magnets' attract to us the forces, the people, the circumstances of life which harmonize with the nature of our dominating thoughts."

—Napoleon Hill (author)

All the great men in history were successful because of their optimistic attitude. An idea conceived in their minds was converted into reality by their belief that they can make it come true. Scientists like Albert Einstein, Thomas Alva Edison, and Homi Jehangir Bhabha could change the world by their extraordinary work because they chased their dreams. Mahatma Gandhi, Nelson Mandela, and Martin Luther King Jr were able to revolutionise the world around them because they believed in the power of righteousness. Distinguished personalities like Rabindranath Tagore, Lata Mangeshkar, Sachin Tendulkar, Serena Williams, etc., were able to spread the glory of their skills throughout the world because of the belief they had in themselves. When these people could make significant contributions to the whole world, can't you make some contributions to the life you have been blessed with?

If you have an idea, faith, and the will to win, you can be the captain of this intangible force within you. As Charles F. Haanel said aptly in his book *The Mastery Key System*,

"This is true because we must 'be' before we can 'do,' and we can 'do' only to the extent which we 'are', and what we 'are' depends upon what we 'think.'"

Have you ever come across thoughts in your mind such as "She is lucky to have a wealthy husband" or "He is lucky to be boss's favourite because of which he gets promoted easily" or "My friend is lucky enough to come first every time without studying enough"? This list can go on and on for many of you! In reality, all these lucky ones in your life are not really that lucky. Things come their way easily because consciously or unconsciously, their thoughts are in tune with what they want from life. They are the ones who think and act positively to achieve their aims. They do not believe or talk about the negativity surrounding them and hence, encounter less of it. Whether you are aware of this fact or not, their thoughts are focused on what they want in life and then working towards those objectives.

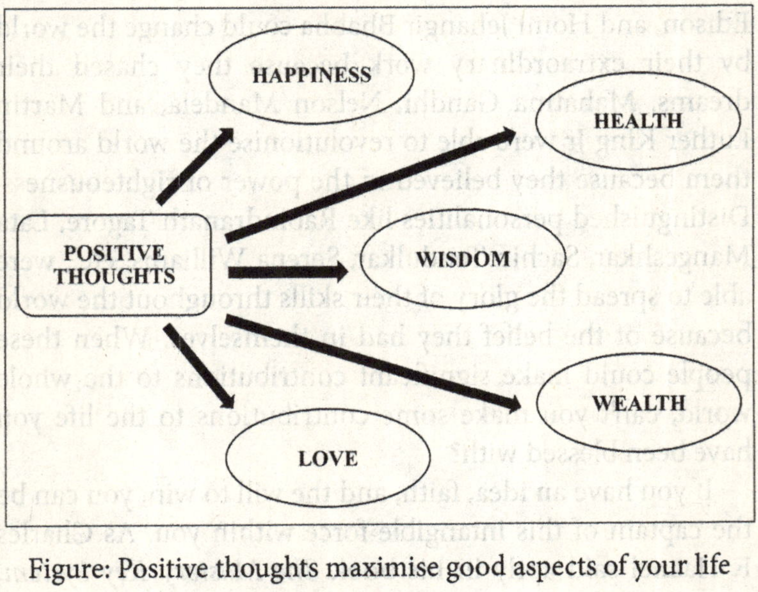

Figure: Positive thoughts maximise good aspects of your life

A good thought can draw more good thoughts into your mind. When your optimistic approach attracts your desired goals, it leads to motivation and happiness. These emotions fuel your mind once again for positive thinking. Thus, a never-ending cycle of positivity will start in your life. Thoughts about wealth will replicate wealth. Thoughts about being broke will replicate being broke. If you want to become rich, then thoughts about money, abundance, wealth, and luxury should be on your mind. As it is said, "In the thought world, birds of a feather flock together."

But you have to be clear about what is it that your heart really wants. Is it love, money, or a promotion? Or is it good health, peace of mind, qualifying an exam, or taking care of your family? What is it? Ask yourself. Once you know it, think about achieving it in a dedicated manner. Think about how happy it will make you. Think how different your life will be after having it. Here are some tips:

- Instead of sickness, think of health.
- Instead of poverty, think of richness.
- Instead of distrust, think of trust.
- Instead of loneliness, think of love.
- Instead of war, think of peace.
- Instead of failure, think of victory.

You will come across ample examples of thought-power in your life. My friend Mira is a great manifestor. She knows what she wants. She got admission into the course of her choice and performed excellently. Then she bagged a high-salaried job at a reputed company. Her goal after college was to pursue her doctorate abroad. With an optimistic attitude and efforts in that direction, she got a call from a foreign university willing to take her as a doctorate fellow with a full scholarship. Today, Mira is out there fulfilling her dreams.

Now, you must be wondering whether it is that easy to practise optimistic thinking. Well, it takes some time since your brain has been trained to look at the problematic aspects and negativity. But with some effort from your side, you can rewire your brain towards having a positive approach. A dedicated plan for changing your thinking pattern has been shared in the chapters to come, but to start with, think along a positive track. It will make you feel bright, buoyant, joyful, and courageous to proceed towards your dreams.

Some Research:

- The Nun Study on Positivity: In a 2001 study at the University of Kentucky, researchers examined autobiographies of 180 catholic nuns, written in 1930. The texts were scored based on emotional content, and the surviving nuns were contacted. Through various statistical analyses, it was concluded that the nuns who displayed a positive approach in their autobiographies written in early adulthood were the ones with the highest longevity, six decades later.

- Life Satisfaction and Positivity: In a study on the Korean population published in *Yonsei Medical Journal* in 2007, the participants provided information on their positive thinking, demography, and life satisfaction. A directly proportional relationship was established between positive thinking and life satisfaction.

The empirical study of the data revealed that positive thinking enhanced the life satisfaction of the participants, irrespective of their demographic disparities. Thus, demographics alone do not determine the level of life satisfaction; a positive attitude also plays a significant role.

Negative Mindset: A Road towards Despair

"Good thoughts bear good fruit; bad thoughts bear bad fruit - and man is his own gardener."
—James Allen (author)

Have you ever wondered why optimists have things working out for them while pessimists find that omens and bad luck keep following them in everything they do? Like nuclear energy, which can be used to light up or destroy, your thought-energy also has the same effect. Every moment, life gives you a choice—whether to light up or crash down.

According to research, up to 95% of what we think is a repetition of our previous day thoughts. Out of these 95% repetitive thoughts, 70% are negative! Thus, the mind tends to easily visualise negative conditions of discord, resentment, despair, etc., unconsciously because these are the uppermost thoughts ruling your mind at any given time, until replaced.

Each day, you continue to engage in this negative mental chatter without even realising how it is damaging you mentally and physically. This tendency is sometimes called negative dominance. It can be demonstrated through an exercise where one notes down his or her mental chatter through a specified period. You can try it for yourself. You will be surprised by the negative dominance in your thoughts.

A single negative thought about an experience or a person can trigger a series of negative emotions within you. These emotions amplify your grief, causing your mind to dive into a pool of other such unpleasant thought-situations. And as you keep recalling such situations, you get stuck deeper and deeper in this cycle of negativity.

Most of the time, you keep complaining about the same situations over and over again like "My boss is a freak", "Oh . . . I will miss the bus again", "I do not have enough time", "Why does Tia keep talking to me like that?", "Why do guys ditch me?", "My children drain the hell out of me", "I can never save enough", "Groceries are expensive", etc. Well, this list is almost always never-ending. If your thoughts and emotions are pessimistic, you attract similar levels of negativity into your life in the form of people, situations, or things. When you wake up in the morning, grumpy about something or the other, you can notice more such things coming your way throughout the day.

Your thoughts and actions have an energy signature. Everything out there in the universe that matches your thoughts' energy frequency will get attracted into your reality. You might think, "I did not attract that bankruptcy into my life." Although unpleasant to hear, I have to say, "Yes, you did!" At a deeper level of your consciousness, you have attracted all the things that you get in your life, even the bad spouse or an irritating boss or a huge debt.

Let's analyse this further with an example. Whenever you are in a rush to catch the metro to work, you either forget to take some documents or even your house keys. And once you are on the road, you cannot find a cab to the metro station. Then you sigh, "Oh God! Why does this always happen whenever I am late?" Well, your high anxiety and the hurry to deal with the lack of time created what was predominant in your mind at that time. And do you know what that was? It was the fear of getting late. So, your mind, which is unable to differentiate between 'do' and 'do not', just acted to make you late.

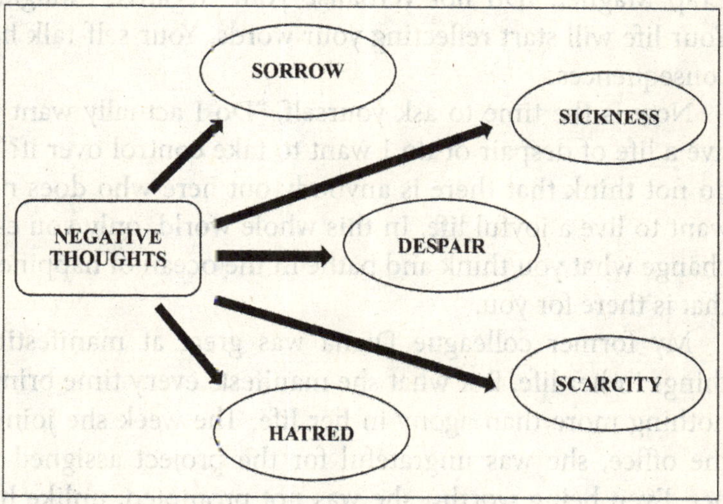

Figure: Negative thoughts maximise bad aspects of your life

Thoughts of despair, anxiety, fear, discomfort, sadness, grief, and scarcity will bring more of that into your life. Many a time, people talk and think about the situations that they do not want in their life. This can be due to fear, a complaining attitude, or victim-mentality. But having grim and gloomy thoughts about your future and talking about them invite all those situations into your life that should be actually forbidden. This not only ruins your future but also makes your present miserable.

If you keep reminding yourself things like "I am not worthy enough" or "I will not qualify for the game/exam" or "I will always be lonely" or "I am always betrayed" or "I do not have enough money" and so on, then believe me, all such situations of hopelessness will keep returning to you again and again. This has been best expressed in words by T. Harv Eker in his book, *Secrets of Millionaire Mind,* when he said, "When you complain, you become a living, breathing Crap Magnet." Do not verbalise your negative thoughts. Your life will start reflecting your words. Your self-talk has consequences.

Now is the time to ask yourself, "Do I actually want to live a life of despair or do I want to take control over it?" I do not think that there is anybody out here who does not want to live a joyful life. In this whole world, only you can change what you think and bathe in the ocean of happiness that is there for you.

My former colleague Diana was great at manifesting things in her life. But what she manifests every time brings nothing more than agony in her life. The week she joined the office, she was ungrateful for the project assigned to her. Even being worthy, she was not promoted, unlike her teammates. She never got along well with her boss. At home, her relationship with her husband was in turmoil.

Feelings of despair in her mind were reflected in her conversations and affected her work. Since the day we met, I have always found her lamenting about her career and relationships. Even before joining the office, she feared that she would not get along well with everyone. When she was getting married, she always feared not getting enough love in her relationships. She created in her life all that she actually never wanted. Her self-sabotaging thoughts compromised her happiness. Thus, it is important to remember that by talking about the unwelcoming situations in your life, you are actually welcoming them into your life. So, stop and pause! Use your brain to decide what to think and then proceed.

Your thoughts shape your character, behaviour, and health. Neuroscientist Dr Caroline Leaf has shared a shocking fact in her book, *Who Switched Off My Brain*. She writes, "Research shows that around 87% of illnesses can be attributed to our thought life, and approximately 13% to diet, genetics, and environment. Studies conclusively link more chronic diseases (also known as lifestyle diseases) to an epidemic of toxic emotions in our culture. These toxic emotions can cause migraines, hypertension, strokes, cancer, skin problems, diabetes, infections, and allergies, just to name a few." Thus, it is evident that negative thoughts are not only poisonous for your success, but they also affect your body. The chemicals released due to negative emotions change the body's environment in some unhealthy way, which makes you sick.

Today, you struggle so much in a mesh of negative thoughts because, till now, you have left them unchecked. But,you can change the pattern of your thoughts by will. You can create and change whatever you want by the force of will acting on your thoughts. No one can do this for you. The good news is that with awareness and some practise, you can alter your thinking pattern.

Authors Esther Hicks and Jerry Hicks describe the role of this force of will in their book, *Ask and It Is Given*. According to them, "There is no condition so severe that you cannot reverse it by choosing different thoughts. However, choosing different thoughts requires focus and practise. If you continue to focus as you have been, to think as you have been, and to believe as you have been, then nothing in your experience will change."

So much information on the importance of positive

thinking can be overwhelming for some of you. There might be questions gushing in your mind presently, like "How to change my thinking?", "Where to start from?", "How to strengthen my will to talk positive?", etc. Do not worry. A positive thought is far more powerful than a negative one, and you should not be terrified with this knowledge that you have gained regarding thought-power. In the sections to come, you will come face to face with methods that will help you change your thought pattern by feeding your subconscious mind with desired thoughts and then attracting your desired results by following the three-step success formula listed in Chapter 4.

Becoming a Proactive Thinker

> *"I believe that everyone chooses how to approach life. If you're proactive, you focus on preparing. If you're reactive, you end up focusing on repairing."*
> —John C. Maxwell (author)

Being proactive means being in control of the situations rather than just responding to what is happening around you. The same applies to proactive creation through proactive thinking. Being a proactive thinker is the essence of this book as well as the theme around which the whole book revolves. Being proactive in taking control of your reality depends on harnessing the thought-power proactively. Take command on your own and replicate your desires into reality rather than responding to your reality. It is the first step towards the use of thought-power. You have to establish a conscious connection with your thoughts and emotions so as to create your life deliberately.

Whatever you observe in your daily life—money, house, love, etc.—generates thoughts and feelings on those aspects, as per your consideration. For example, when you spot a leakage in the ceiling of your house, you may think of the shortage of budget or time which has delayed the repair work. This observation spoils your mood and may lead to some other unwanted attractions or creations. Being a proactive thinker helps you deal with such mood spoilers. By intentional and deliberate thinking, you can think and feel as per your desires and not as per your observances of your current state, in case they are contradictory. Ignore the unwanted and wilfully think about the wanted. Remember, your desired results will be in proportion to your proactive thinking.

Today, you are the product of your past thinking pattern; tomorrow, you will be the product of your current thinking pattern. Therefore, each second of the day, when you get a chance to think, think intentionally and proactively. Your focused thoughts have to be like a polarised light . . . all your thought-energy should be coherent in one frame. When this happens, your life will shine brilliantly.

Proactive thinking is conscious-thinking, where you take charge of your thinking habits. The four steps to becoming a proactive thinker are:

1. **Knowledge of thought-power:** To use something efficiently, you should know about it. This is what we have been talking about in Chapter 1.
2. **Developing faith in thought-power by understanding its history and science:** This equips you better as you are no longer sceptical about it. You will get to know about it in Chapter 2.

3. **Developing an unhampered belief system:** Here, we try to change the underlying thoughts buried in your subconscious mind. By removing old thinking patterns, you make way for new and better one's. You will get a deeper understanding of this in Chapter 3.
4. **Best possible utilisation of thought-power by becoming a proactive thinker:** In Chapter 4, 5, 6, and 7, you will learn how to make conscious efforts to change your reality by applying the three-step success formula.

Your thoughts bring to you, your reality in two different ways. Sometimes, you attract the change you want to see by changing your subconscious beliefs, neurological networks of your brain, habits, behaviours, patterns, and actions. While sometimes, you need to cause a ripple in the energy of the universe around you. It depends upon what you desire. The coming chapters will prepare you for both changing your beliefs and manifesting from this energy of the universe.

Chapter 2
Exploring the Truth

"What we know is a drop, what we don't know is an ocean."
—Sir Isaac Newton (physicist)

Anyone who has ever tried to change the course of knowledge has always been ridiculed and rejected at first. Some examples of it being Christopher Columbus, Nicolaus Copernicus, Galileo Galilei, etc. In our easygoing life, when something huge, amazing, and strange comes our way, we are often in the habit of discounting that knowledge as supernatural, mystical, or forbidden. But so that you do not consider the facts shared in this book as some fairy-tale ideas, this chapter becomes an imperative part of our learning process.

Until a few years ago, even I wasn't too eager to accept this concept of thought-power. After all, it was turning my whole set of beliefs upside down. I was unable to believe that things are totally under my control and I remained a sceptic until I explored numerous historical and scientific facts behind thought-power. Therefore, considering various types of readers out there, I decided not to jump directly to the process of harnessing thought-power. To proceed in that direction, this chapter is dedicated to the history and science behind thought-power.

In Chapter 1, I discussed the extraordinary capabilities we possess as human beings. But some of us like analysing and comprehending everything before believing it. Such people like to wait for some scientific explanations, evidence, and experiments in support of the existence of thought-power. If you are one of them, you would be completely justified in disagreeing with the concept of thought-power in the first instance. After all, if thought-power rules the world of human beings, then why are so many people unaware about it? Also, if it is such an integral part of our lives then why is it not taught in schools? And so, the doubts ramble on and on. However, as you move deeper into this chapter, you will find answers to the doubts regarding the efficacy of thought-power.

For those readers who already agree and understand this concept, this section will further strengthen your belief and the desired use of your thought-power will amplify. Let me tell you from my own experience that all my sluggishness in applying thought-power vanished once I realised that it is not just some 'be-positive breeze' that comes up every now and then, led by some motivational guru. For all those people who were totally unfamiliar with the concept until now or are sceptical about its worth, this section has an immense potential of clearing your doubts. You will explore that thought-power has always been there and it was just that you were not aware of it.

Why is belief important? Until you believe, you will not have faith. And once you decide not to have faith in this concept, the whole point of reading the book will be missed out. I have come across a few people who refused to accept that thought-power governs our lives. So, if they remain in denial, will they ever be able to harness this power in a proactive manner? No, never! The beauty of the effectiveness of thought-power lies in the simple fact that until you believe in it with all your heart and mind, you cannot use it intentionally.

Your life is not concrete or rock solid; it is a flexible, free-flowing river of energy whose path can be changed by using the correct technique. This is what you will come to know in the coming sections. Exploring the history and science behind your thought-power will be an awakening towards an inner world of greater abundance.

Let's explore the truth.

Step 1: Four Stages of Competence Model of Learning

To begin, let me quote the famous 20th-century astronomer Carl Sagan, "Somewhere, something incredible is waiting to be known." What remains unknown can only be known by an explorer with an open mind. The competence model of learning is a good start to understand what we know and don't know. This model consists of 4 pillars which are as follows:

- **Unconscious Incompetence**

  You are unaware of the existence or relevance of a new skill, concept, behaviour, etc. For example, the Sentinelese tribe, indigenous to the Andaman Islands, is unaware of the fact that a vehicle called car exists.

- **Conscious Incompetence**

  You are aware of the existence or relevance of the concerned concept but fall short in its application. For example, when one of the Sentinelese people is brought into a city, he becomes aware of the moving vehicle on the roads called car but is incompetent to use it.

- **Conscious Competence**

  You are aware of the existence or relevance of the concerned concept and can apply it with conscious efforts and concentration. For example, under guidance, the Sentinelese person learns to use and control the car with conscious efforts.

- **Unconscious Competence**

  You are aware of the existence or relevance of the concerned concept and can apply it without any conscious efforts as if it is second nature. For example, after many months, with daily practise, driving a car becomes an unconscious act for the Sentinelese person, just like fishing, during which he can talk to his friend while performing the act.

I brought this point up to show the reality of where we exist today in terms of our knowledge about the human mind and universe. All the stars, galaxies, planets, and space known to scientists comprise only 4.9% of what is actually present! Do you see the amount of unconscious incompetence here? After more than 200,000 years of Homo sapiens on the planet Earth, we just know as little as 4.9% of this universe! So, do not boast that you know everything and do not assert that science has discovered everything. There is no dead end to the knowledge we can explore out of this observable universe which has a diameter of 93 billion light years or 879 followed by 21 zeros in kilometres!

If we compare all that we know till now with all that is present, then a justifiable analogy to represent this difference would be the comparison of the height of a dot with that of a six-foot-tall human being. With each scientific generation, when we start believing that this is the end to all that can be known, nature surprises us with some richer modes of expression, leaving us in complete awe.

In respect to thought-power, if you are lying in the incompetence area, then remove the veils so that you can take a step towards being consciously competent and from there to become unconsciously competent. Expanding the frame of your knowledge will help you build your desirable life.

Step 2: Types of Learners

From the above discussion, it can be concluded that until now, many of you were in the unconscious incompetent zone regarding thought-power. But the fact is that this force has always been there even if you were unaware of its existence. Now, as you come into the zone of conscious incompetency, we will try to identify the kind of person you are when it comes to knowing and applying new ideas, theories, techniques, etc. There are basically four different types of people in this respect, as listed below (This differentiation has been referred from a blog published by Mindvalley Academy).

- **Non-Believer**

  This group is unable to accept any theory or phenomenon that cannot be explained by Newtonian physics. Any scientific evidence that discards Newtonian physics is unacceptable to them.

- **Sceptic**

  This group has a high regard for scientific facts. They accept only those facts that are accompanied by scientific evidence. They do not like to exploit concepts that cannot be proven by equations.

- **Cautious Believer**

  This group is open-minded. They are ready to trust and harness the benefits of a fact after looking at the proof. They accept new knowledge and facts based on scientific evidence, testimonies, reliable sources, or references without being too conservative.

- **True Believer**

  This group believes in every kind of new knowledge provided to them without touching upon any proof. They are convinced easily. Their blind-faith attitude is generally of less help and, sometimes, can cost them.

Now, you have to judge for yourself which category you are in when it comes to understanding and applying thought-power for your benefit. Understanding your own mindset is important if you want to dive deep into the ocean of immense power that you hold within. Also, coming out of the old-school thinking will give you a new perspective of looking at yourself and your life. Until you believe in the importance and presence of thought-power in your world, no books or audios or teachers can transform your life. Without full participation from your side, I cannot show you the way of living the life you have been searching for. When you open yourself up to the possibilities out there, only then will miracles start to happen. Set aside all scepticism for the time being and just flow with the current of this book. Cherish the hidden power that you just came to know about and make plans to benefit from it in several positive ways.

History of Thought-Power

"The truth is that the universe has been answering you all of your life, but you cannot receive the answers unless you are aware."

—Rhonda Byrne (author)

Few great men from the past understood the competence of their thoughts, and this resulted in their greatness or success in ruling the world. Today, due to the generous efforts of great teachers and practitioners of thought-power, we have this opportunity to understand and apply this concept in our lives.

Tracing the history of some universal truth is a challenging task. It may have persisted from the time the universe was created, with or without our awareness. Nonetheless, I have made some efforts to bring to you the background of thought-power.

All religions refer to the existence of thought-power. The word 'thought-power' may not have been used directly, but references to mind, faith, soul, and karma in the ancient texts make it clear that our highly evolved ancestors wanted this truth to be conveyed to the future generations. In the Hindu scripture, Bhagavad Gita, the author Veda-Vyasa writes about the conversations on karma, faith, and eternal soul which happened between Krishna and the Pandava prince, Arjuna. The teachings in the Bhagavad Gita indicate that we are responsible for our actions, man is made up of the faith he has, and the soul cannot be created or destroyed.

In the Buddhist scripture *Dhammapada,* Gautama Buddha gave clear insights on thought-power to his disciples when he said, "All that we are is the result of what we have thought: it is founded on our thoughts, it is made up of our thoughts. If a man speaks or acts with an evil thought, pain follows him, as the wheel follows the foot of the ox that draws the carriage. If a man speaks or acts with a pure thought, happiness follows him, like a shadow that never leaves him." (Translated by Max Muller)

Also, throughout the Holy Bible, in the teachings of Jesus, you can see references to thought-power. For example, "Therefore I say unto you, what things soever ye desire, when ye pray, believe that ye receive them, and ye shall have them." (Mark 11:24, KJV)

The proverb from the Holy Bible, "As you sow, so shall you reap," also refers to the importance of karma. All your inner and outer situations are the results of the seeds that you have sown in your mind. Whatever you think and do, you get back in your life, sooner or later. Every second of your life is unfolding as a response to your thoughts. It is a 'give out' and 'take in' relationship. Whatever you will give out to the energy of the universe, you will have to take it in at some point of time. That is the cycle of karma.

The Hermetica, the Egyptian-Greek wisdom texts which dates back to the 2nd and 3rd centuries CE, has listed seven spiritual principles that govern the universe. These seven Hermetic principles for self-mastery taught by Hermes Trismegistus include the Principle of Vibration (nothing is still, everything in the universe is in a state of constant vibration), Principle of Mentalism (All is mind), Principle of Cause-Effect (everything that happens has a cause/law behind it, which may or may not go unnoticed). These principles constitute the modern-day understanding of thought-power. Many of these Hermetic principles have now been proved true by quantum physics.

In circa 391 BCE, Plato stated in his longest dialogue,

Laws, "Such as are the trend of our desires and the nature of our souls, just such each of us becomes." Also, in his Socratic dialogue *Republic*, he stated that like always attracts like.

But as time passed, a significant two-class system emerged in society—Religion and Science. And the idea that 'a divine spark exists within each human being' suited neither of them. Also, as mentioned before, the very fact of its extraordinary potential made thought-power a daunting concept to be popularised and the sects which believed in the interconnectedness of mind and matter were forced to reside back. All these factors brought a long gap in the passing down of the knowledge of thought-power to successive generations and only in a handful of groups—alchemists, mystics, shamans, yogis, etc.—this knowledge endured.

From the Renaissance period to the industrial age, many philosophers, physicians, historians, and authors emerged who started the work of reviving this ancient secret. Marsilio Ficino, Count Mirandola, Heinrich Cornelius Agrippa, Giordano Bruno, Philippus Hohenheim, Emanuel Swedenborg, Franz Anton Mesmer, Alphonse-Louis Constant are just a few names that made a significant contribution to this movement.

The 19th century saw further growth of the concept of thought-power due to the works of Phineas Parkhurst Quimby. Though Quimby never used the term directly, he is now believed to be the founder of the New Thought movement. He introduced the concept of Mental Healing. In his words, "The fact is, there is nothing of us but belief. It is the whole capital and stock in trade of man. It is all that can be changed, and embraces everything man has made or ever will make."

In 1877, Helena Blavatsky, co-founder of the Theosophical Society, used the specific term 'Law of Attraction' for the first time in her book *Isis Unveiled: A Master-Key to the Mysteries of Ancient and Modern Science and Theology.*

From the late 19th century onwards, the concept kept on gaining popularity in the form of the New Thought movement which talked about the power of positive thinking. This idea was spread by the works of authors like Prentice Mulford (*Thoughts are Things*), Ralph Waldo Trine (*Character-Building Thought-power*), James Allen (*As a Man Thinketh*), Thomas Toward (*The Edinburgh Lectures on Mental Science*), Wallace D. Wattles (*The Science of Getting Rich*), William Walker Atkinson (*Thought Vibration*), Bruce MacLelland (*Prosperity Through Thought Force*), Charles F. Haanel (*The Master-Key System*), and Ernest Holmes (*The Science of Mind*), etc. In 1937, Napoleon Hill wrote the first bestseller on this subject, *Think and Grow Rich*. The book remains as one of the most successful contributions to the literature on thought-power till now.

The 20th and 21st centuries have witnessed many great authors and researchers who have contributed to the concept of thought-power in spiritual and scientific terms. Their efforts have spread awareness among a much broader audience. The mainstream publicity of the concept came from the efforts of Rhonda Byrne, who produced the documentary, *The Secret,* in 2006 and later authored a book by the same name.

To gain in-depth knowledge of the origin of the concept of thought-power, mind-matter interactions, and consciousness, *Real Magic* by Dr Dean Radin, chief scientist at the Institute of Noetic Sciences, is a suggested read. Dr Radin very well portraits the history of this concept (which he calls 'Force of Will' in his book) back to historical ages.

Many works of literature suggest that in the past, the knowledge and harnessing of thought-power had been prominent in the Eastern cultures. The irony remains that our culture, which once played an important role in identifying the power of our thoughts and consciousness, is lagging far behind in applying thought-power today.

The words chosen to express this concept of thought-power may vary from text to text. Many different terms have been used to address this concept like positive thinking, new thought, mental science, practical metaphysics, mind power, the force of will, etc., but the essence remains the same, which is 'thoughts create your reality'.

And in whatever form suitable, this truth should be conveyed to every generation. Everyone on this planet has the right to know their self-worth. Everyone has the right to be happy, abundant, prosperous, and in good health. This reminds me of the words of Henry David Thoreau, "Rather than love, than money, than fame, give me the truth."

The Science of Thought-Power

> *"The day science begins to study non-physical phenomena, it will make more progress in one decade than in all the previous centuries of its existence. To understand the true nature of the universe, one must think it in terms of energy, frequency, and vibration."*
>
> —Nikola Tesla (physicist)

After going through the history of thought-power, let us now dive a little deeper in this section to understand how it works. Thought-power is not a mystical phenomenon, but rather is a complex science with its solid roots penetrating into the concepts of quantum physics, which in itself is an ocean which has not been completely explored till now. Quantum physics is a field which is very difficult to comprehend due to the complicated concepts it delves in. So, if you find it difficult to understand the following topics, then do not worry at all. Understanding the detailed science involved in thought-power is a demanding task which is still under research and beyond the scope of this book. But it is essential that you take away with you the essence of this chapter.

I am no physicist to talk about the theories of quantum physics and keeping this in mind, I won't dare to explain it in detail except to the point that my readers from different backgrounds get a glimpse of the connecting link between thought-power and science. So, let's start by defining a few terms that will help you better understand the hypothesis put forward by scientists to explain thought-power.

❖ Matter

Matter is a substance that has mass and occupies some space and it can be broken down into atoms. Each atom further constitutes subatomic particles called protons, neutrons, and electrons. Every matter present around us is made of these basic subatomic particles. Our bodies have the basic chemical composition of proteins, carbohydrates, and fats. These chemicals, in turn, are made of atomic and subatomic particles. This concludes that at the most fundamental level, our bodies are made up of an infinitely large number of subatomic particles.

❖ Classical Physics

Classical physics, sometimes known as Newtonian physics, is the study of matter at macroscopic levels. It deals with motion, thermodynamics, electromagnetism, and other such properties of matter.

❖ **Quantum Physics**

Quantum physics is also called the 'Physics of Possibilities'. It deals with the fundamental nature of matter at its atomic and subatomic levels. At the subatomic state, matter behaves as both particle and energy. An electron can exist as a wave of energy and as a solid particle. These infinitely minute subatomic particles or energy bundles pose limits to the precision with which quantities can be measured in quantum physics. At such small scales, the well-set principles of classical physics are violated.

❖ **Energy**

Albert Einstein, who was a theoretical physicist and one of the greatest scientists of the millennium, never believed in a traditional God. He once said, "Everyone who is seriously involved in the pursuit of science becomes convinced that a spirit is manifest in the laws of the universe—a spirit vastly superior to that of man, and one in the face of which we with our modest powers must feel humble."

According to quantum physics, everything in this universe is made up of energy and is in a state of constant vibration. From every human being to the book you hold in your hands to the birds flying in the sky to the stars and the space above, everything is energy. This intangible energy force is the basis of all that exists and is flowing everywhere, from one form to another. Also, this energy has a wave pattern with a set frequency and wavelength.

With this information, the line which your biology teacher must have said that 'DNA is the building block of life' can be held to question now. In his book, *The Science of Getting Rich*, Wallace D. Wattles said, "Everything you see on Earth is made from one original substance, out of which all things proceed." If we go deeper, we find that it is the energy which is the building block at the core. You, I, everybody, and everything is a miraculous manifestation of this energy of the universe. All of us around the world, despite our colour, creed, intelligence, opinions, status, etc., are constituents of a single large vibrating field of energy, expressing itself in various forms. These vibrations are beyond our observations as our sensory system is not modelled to perceive them. Energy healer and teacher Jeffrey Allen has said, "You are not a body having energy, you are energy having a physical body."

❖ Observer

Anyone with consciousness—having the ability to think and choose—residing within is an observer. Hence, every human being can be considered as an observer.

❖ Principle of Wave-Particle Duality

This principle states that subatomic particles have dual states of existence. These particles can behave as a particle (matter) or a wave (energy). This means that particles such as electrons can behave like a wave and can be described by a wave function. This can be demonstrated by the reproducible double-slit experiment, which studies the pattern formed by electrons when passed through slits.

❖ Copenhagen Interpretation

It asserts that matter at subatomic levels tends to be in all possible states (particle and wave) at any given time. It is only when the observer observes or measures its states that the particle is forced to choose one finite state. So, unless observed, the particle does not even exist. The observation can be done through a measuring device or in person. The act of observance affects the state that the matter will take after observation. This leads to the debatable topic of whether objective reality exists or not!

❖ **Quantum Superposition**

When the particle is not being observed, it has an infinite potential of being in all possible states. This phenomenon is termed as quantum superposition. A thought experiment by physicist Erwin Schrodinger, called the Schrodinger's Cat Experiment, gives a simple but profound explanation of this concept. It demonstrates how the superposition of states is interrupted by the act of observing.

❖ **Collapse of the Wave**

The total possible quantum states of a particle during quantum superposition constitutes the particle's wave function which is given by Schrodinger's wave equation. When an observer gives attention to any particular quantum state, the other wave functions collapse, i.e. the other states vanish. This reduces the whole scenario of superposition to one single state (particle), which is a well-defined state of finite possibility. The act of observing these energy packets collapses them into matter and affects the outcome or reality.

❖ **Link between Quantum Physics and Thought-Power**

The incapability of present-day science to fully understand the quantum nature of the matter and the complexities of the human brain has led to a few debatable hypotheses to explain the role of the conscious observer in changing reality. Today, the scientists have researched further on the ideas of quantum physics theorised by the pioneers of this field like Max Planck, Louis D. Broglie, Neils Bohr, Erwin Schrodinger, Werner Heisenberg, Wolfgang Pauli, etc. The research work and ideas of authors, scientists, and researchers like Edgar Mitchell, Hal Puthoff, J. B. Rhine, Helmut Schmidt, Robert Jahn, Roger Nelson, Dean Radin, Iann Swann, Rene Peoc'h, Fritjof Capra, William Braud, Elizabeth Targ, William A. Tiller, Karl Pribram, Stuart Hameroff, Jeffery Satinover, Joe Dispenza, Fred Alan Wolf, Amit Goswami, Andrew B. Newberg, to name a few, has led to a concluding hypothesis which tries to understand the role of intentions in changing our day-to-day reality. Their work reflects that thought-power is not some simple positive thinking new age philosophy but rather has a vast scientific background.

From the concept of quantum energy-universe, it is inferred that all matter exists as energy waves. These energy waves of different frequencies and wavelengths have the opportunity to exist in a variety of states at any given time (Copenhagen Interpretation). The moment an observer pays attention through his or her thoughts to a matter (object/situation), its energy waves collapse into the corresponding solid material reality (wave function collapse). Every thought which we had, have, or will have will interact with the ocean of energy waves present around us. Few other research also suggest the role of zero-point field, human consciousness, and the quantum nature of brain in this mind-matter interaction.

Another significant subject to be considered here is of 'choice' which is an important tool possessed by an observer. By choosing an outcome for this moment, this hour, this day, or this life, you can limit the infinite possibilities present in the pool of outcomes. Each decision you make as an observer limits the degree of freedom of random manifestation of the physical system. The reality of your life is in a molten state and can be changed and moulded into some other form by the artistry of your thoughts.

Dr William A. Tiller (professor emeritus of Materials Science and Engineering at Stanford University) explains that the observer is our spirit (intangible eternal energy), which is residing in our four-layered bio-bodysuits (human body). Through his Tiller-Einstein model and psycho-energetic analysis, Dr Tiller traces the entire series of steps of energy manifestation initiated by the energy within us. According to well-known theoretical physicist John Wheeler, mind is involved in the creation of reality and it is not just an observer but rather a 'participant' in the creation of reality. Whether it's the mind that is the observer or the consciousness, the medium through which reality gets its form is our thoughts.

If you want to go deeper into the research concluding the presence of observer-effect in mind-matter interactions, then *The Field* by Lynn MacTaggart, *The Conscious Universe* by Dr Dean Radin, and *Mind to Matter* by Dr Dawson Church are good books to satiate your scientific aptitude. You can also watch *What the Bleep Do We Know*, a documentary or read the book by the same name. It is a compilation of opinions of researchers on the endless possibilities we have for altering our reality.

The energy of the universe works in synchronisation with your thoughts. This concept has designed your past, is designing your present, and will design your future. Whether you are aware of its existence or not, this phenomenon is continuously at work, 24×7. Whatever you are going to radiate out into the universal energy pool, you will process and bring back into your life.

Let me give a very common analogy of radio broadcasting that is frequently used to understand this concept. When you want to hear a song on 98.3 FM, then you tune your radio to that frequency so as to match it with the signals from the broadcasting tower. Till the time your radio is set at 104.0 FM, you will hear what is being played on this frequency and not the one you want, i.e. 98.3 FM. The radio waves from your device and the broadcasting station must match in their frequencies and vibrations, just like your intentions and desired reality. Every time you want a particular reality (things/situations/people) in your life, you need to think the same thoughts.

By now you must be wondering that if thoughts are energy and energy manifests, then why haven't you witnessed this happening around you with the naked eye. The answer to this question lies in the following question: why do you see your friend as a human body and not some glowing energy bundle? This is because our five senses can perceive different spectrums of energy with limitations. Your mind can sense only those things for which it has some internal mapping. This mapping differs from species to species. What we perceive as reality is different for somebody who has another brain mapping of perceiving the energy spectrum.

For example, different species of animals have different levels of energy perception than human beings. Depending on the breed of dog, its sense of smell can be 1000 to 10,000,000 times better than humans. Sometimes, in differently-abled people who cannot see, the brain rewires to enhance the perception by other senses to assist and compensate for the lack of sight.

In her book *E-Squared*, Pam Grout explains this perception idea in a rather entertaining way: "... spinning at a rate of roughly 930 miles per hour. It's (Earth) orbiting the sun at an astonishing 66,486 miles per hour. But unless you just polished off a couple of pitchers of beer, you probably aren't aware of any such movement. That's just one tiny example of how we distort reality."

The Paradigm Shift

"I hope basic science becomes part of general awareness. What now appear as the paradoxes of quantum theory will seem as just common sense to our children's' children."

—Dr Stephen Hawkins (physicist)

It is estimated that the human body is made up of 3.72×10^{13} or 37.2 trillion cells, and a single cell is made up of 100 trillion atoms. So, try calculating the total number of atoms present in your body! These amazingly large number of atoms with their core as energy waves and following the principles of quantum physics can surely result in some enigmatic phenomenon like thought-power.

Research on the exact workings of intentions, mind consciousness, energy, and the universe are still in a nascent and debatable state because of the complexities of the systems involved and the incompetency of the human brain to understand them at this point. But the crucial point to consider is that this research confirms that there is a link between our intentions and our reality.

The scientific process involved in thought-power has been of debate for non-believers because it is so immensely mysterious that it becomes easier to be a non-believer than search and accept the truth. Understanding that which is intangible with the limited tangible means sometimes restricts our intelligence, and we become ignorant of the real fact. In his work titled *Conscious Acts of Creation*, Dr William A Tiller writes, "It is psychologically easier to reject the existence/validity of such data than to go through the difficult process of changing 'hardwired' mental patterns concerning reality." Whether we deny or accept, the universal truth will never change.

Author and journalist Lynne McTaggart says something worth quoting here: "To be a true explorer in science—to follow the unprejudiced lead of pure scientific inquiry—is to be unafraid to propose the unthinkable, and to prove friends, colleagues, and scientific paradigms wrong."

Until quantum physics made its way too firmly in science, all that was invisible and beyond the physical realms was left for religion to understand. Today, the lines of division between spirituality and science are getting blurred as thought-power emerges to be no more a New Age dogma, disapproved by sceptics earlier. It is not magic, mysticism, philosophy, or metaphysics. Although today, the pace of research can't be said to be startling, the scenario is changing with many researchers accepting the connection between invisible energy, mind, and thought-power.

In his book, *The Grand Design*, Dr Stephen Hawking—one of the brightest minds of the century—wrote that for nearly two thousand years, Aristotle's deeply entrenched science paradigms prevailed in the scientific community until it was challenged by people such as Galileo. History is proof that we cannot take anything for granted about the universe and science. In the mid-1500s, Copernicus revolutionised science and religion by discovering that the

Earth is not the centre of the universe. It dealt with a lot of criticism from various groups, but ultimately marked a complete paradigm shift from old beliefs. Similarly, when the Theory of Relativity was proposed by Albert Einstein in the 20th century, it created major turbulence in the scientific community as it replaced many aspects of the then 200-year-old concepts of classical or Newtonian physics.

Today, we may be in a state of conscious incompetency, where we don't know all the details of thought-power. Whether we understand the 'how' of thought-power right now is not important in comparison to the awareness of its existence itself. From the dawn of civilisation, mankind has been using natural phenomenon like sun, winds, and flowing waters, even without knowing how these actually worked until a few 100 years back. Similarly, currently no one knows for sure how phenomena like thought-power work, but that simply does not matter when it comes to utilising them. The truth will survive because it is eternal.

Now is the time to look at science as an open-minded path leading towards knowing the unknown, rather than constricting our viewpoint around what our eyes can see. Thereafter, when you will stand in front of a mirror, you will admire that the intangible and invisible is present within you and is more powerful and beautiful than anything outside. Dr William A. Tiller calls these super-physical abilities as 'actualising our latent abilities by becoming more coherent and conscious'. The key to the lock lies in your hand, and you have been looking for it in the outside world. It is the jockey who always holds the halter and no one else!

Some mind-boggling research and experiments on thought-power, intentions, and human consciousness have been shared below:

❖ Thought-Power in Action

Dr William Tiller, professor emeritus at Stanford University, has conducted many experiments to demonstrate the effect of human intentions on inorganic and organic or living and non-living things. One of his interesting experiments was about raising the ATP production in fruit fly by the power of specific intentions. His team designed a lab experiment where they focused their desired intentions (of increased ATP production) on a box. This imprinted box together with a control box was sent 1,500 miles away to a different laboratory in Minnesota. The two boxes were kept in two separate cages of fruit flies. The fruit flies in the cage with the imprinted box had increased ATP and an improved genealogical line. These results were significant enough to be ruled by chance alone.

❖ Effect of Human Intentions on Machines

Dr Robert Jahn of the Princeton University started a PEAR programme to look into the interaction of mind with matter (machine). With the help of others in this field, he came up with a machine called Random Number Generator whose task was to produce randomly, two numbers—1 and 0. The chances of this were 50% just like tossing a coin and getting heads or tails. The test participants were expected to direct their intentions to produce more of either 1 or 0. Under strict laboratory protocols, these RNG experiments were carried for a period of 12 years with nearly 2.5 million trials concluding that human intentions were able to direct the result of the machine. Similar experimental results have been replicated by different labs throughout the world.

❖ Intentional Healing, Distant Healing, and the Power of Prayer

Science has shown that intentional thoughts can produce healing effects on the subject even at a distance. This is attributed to the strong electromagnetic coherent energy waves emitted by the healer (like Qigong masters). Reiki healers have been pictured to show strong laser-like energy emitting from their hands while healing. The spiritual name for this energy is aura, while science calls it biophoton emissions. Dr Fritz-Albert Popp discovered these highly coherent energy emissions to be commonly present in plants, animals, and humans.

A classic laboratory experiment on healing power was carried out by Dr William Braud of Mind Science Foundation, Texas. He tested the reduction in the hemolysis of red blood cells when subjected to visualisation and intentional healing. A significant number of positive results of these double-blinded placebo studies indicated that the healing was not a matter of chance alone. (Dr William Braud, 1994; Dr Daniel J. Benor, 2000)

Controlled laboratory experiments conducted by Randolph Byrd, Elisabeth Targ, and Fred Sicher confirmed the fact that various healing modalities have improved outcomes on the patient. The astonishing part is that the art of intentional healing is not limited to a few gifted healers. Ordinary people have been shown to provide intentional healing during experiments designed to verify the same. (MAHI Study by W. Harris)

❖ Telepathy in Plants

It has been scientifically confirmed that plants can respond to our thought-power via some sort of quantum communication. Research by Cleve Backster (discoverer of telepathy in plants) and Dr Fritz-Albert Popp (biophysicist) led to the emergence of this concept. Projection of positive and loving thoughts towards plants can make them thrive more vigorously.

❖ Effect of Thoughts on Water

Many experiments have been conducted to study the power of thoughts to influence water. Popular research conducted by Dr Masaru Emoto (*The Hidden Messages in Water*, 2004) concluded that water samples that were focused with positive thoughts (like love and gratitude) produced symmetric, well-designed, and aesthetically beautiful ice crystals. Conversely, those subjected to negative intentions (like hatred) produced asymmetric and unattractive crystals. Since 70% of the human body is water, just imagine the effect your thoughts can have on your body.

❖ The Global Consciousness Project

This project originated at the PEAR Lab of Princeton University. It collects global data from physical random number generators located in up to 70 host sites around the world. It aims to examine the subtle correlation between human consciousness and global activities that engage our hearts and minds. The project records many results throughout the year and its major recordings have been seen during the 9/11 attack, tsunamis, deaths of public figures, presidential inaugurations, etc.

❖ Placebo Effect

"A beneficial effect produced by a placebo drug or treatment, which cannot be attributed to the properties of the placebo itself and must, therefore, be due to the patient's belief in that treatment." The Internet is flooded with various experiments done to test the placebo effect wherein the patients who believe that they are receiving the right drug or surgery (placebo medication/surgery) get equally cured like their counterparts who have undergone the prescribed medication or surgery. To understand how you alone can heal yourself by your thoughts, I recommend reading the books *You Can Heal Your Life* by Louis L. Hay and *You are the Placebo* by Dr Joe Dispenza. The opposite of placebo is the nocebo effect, where negative thoughts harm your health and body.

Thought-power cannot just be used to transform our lives but also the world at large. Collective positive thoughts and healing intentions can make the world a better place to live in. Your God lies within you. You just have to look inside with all faith. Eckhart Tolle, a spiritual author who was listed as the most spiritually influential living people by the Watkins Review in 2011, once said, "You are this universe experiencing itself, very briefly, as a human."

If you want to try out some easy thought experiments for yourself, go through the book *E-squared* by Pam Grout. The book is a compilation of nine easy-to-do experiments to test your thought-power. If you still want to be a sceptic, you will have it as your reality. However, your scepticism can never prevent thought-power from actualising. The loss you will incur is that you will never try to be a positive proactive thinker.

Why Is Manifestation Challenging?

"The only limit to your impact is your imagination & commitment."
—Tony Robbins (author)

From all the history and science of thought-power which you have been reading up till now, you might be thinking things like "Why can't I manifest my desired intentions to reach my peak potential?" or "Why can't I remove corruption, war, and poverty from this world through my intentions?" Well, you can make intentional use of your thought-power, depending upon how expertly and independently you are using them.

Since, through this book I want the readers to understand the complete know-how of using thought-power, it is important to bring this point up. This idea is not dreamland magic. It works on certain laws and thus has certain restriction. Few factors that act as a break in the free-flow movement of your thoughts are summed up below:

❖ **Subconscious Beliefs**

At the upper surface, it may seem to you that you have a particular desire and thus an intention towards achieving it. But at deeper levels of your subconscious mind, your beliefs can be contradictory of your desire. When such clashes occur between your thoughts and beliefs, it becomes difficult to manifest your desires. You may think something but perform just the opposite!

How to overcome this setback is dealt with in the next chapter. Once you understand the role of your brain, mind, beliefs, thoughts and feelings, it will surely get you on track to create your reality. Further, Chapters 4 through 7 will help you in rebuilding your subconscious blueprint by following the various processes listed in these chapters.

❖ Hardwired Neural Networks

The brain cells have a neural network—networks of brain cells called neurons—corresponding to each of your behaviour, beliefs, memories, emotional-identity, actions, etc. All that which you keep doing regularly is stored in these brain circuits for easy access the next time. These hardwired, well-programmed neural circuits of the brain make you repeat your past behaviours and actions. Thus, when you act similar to your past, you manifest your past and not a different future.

Throughout the book, you will find various tips on how you can start the journey of becoming a new you by breaking unwanted networks and forming new ones. From shattering old beliefs (Chapter 3) to following the three-step success formula (Chapters 4 through 7), you will be provided with all the tools towards changing your neural network to align with the process of manifestation.

❖ Power of Observance

As you have seen till now, everything depends on your power to think or observe. The power to observe is the capacity possessed by all human beings. But today, in this fast-paced world of technology, pollution, population, consumerism, and wastage, you have lost your power of observation. You are so distracted by the outward show that rarely do you sit and contemplate in order to access your power. In the midst of the necessities of daily survival, long-standing violent media news, overwhelming competition in life, and the rat race at work, gaining moments of focus and peace is like a far-fetched vacation idea.

The monkey-mind keeps jumping from one appointment to the other. The key for a successful application of thought-power lies in undivided attention on your desired thought. But this is not happening! You are unable to concentrate on one thought for barely a few seconds. In such a case, the goal of proactive observation becomes a distant milestone to reach.

What is the remedy then? Meditation is one of the best ways in my opinion. When you meditate, you develop mindfulness which is the ability to live in the present moment. Meditation does not completely silence your monkey-mind, but it can bring down the noise to an extent that is required for good observation. In a nutshell, meditation boosts the ability to stay focused. Chapter 6 of the book talks in detail about how you can start your daily meditation ritual.

Further, you have to make your thoughts revolve around things that truly matter to you. By practices such as affirmation, visualisation, paying gratitude, action plans, etc., you will have a better command on your thoughts. Your focus will be less on random stuff and more on what you want from life. These methods (shared in Chapter 5, 6, and 7) to stay focused and being positive will assist mindfulness in your life.

❖ Reality Inertia

Dr Dean Radin of the Institute of Noetic Sciences explains reality inertia as the tendency of the energy of the universe to remain in a state of stability by balancing or rebounding itself to gain this stability. Creating your reality depends on your intentions but yours aren't the only intentions. You are not a single human being with this power; there are 7.8 billion human consciousness ruling the planet Earth. So, when your intention creates a little bend in the energy of the universe here, that bend may not be preferred at the other end and you may be pushed back.

So, how can you overcome this? And how can you make your intentions or thoughts powerful enough to create and maintain a change in the energy of the universe around you, such that it doesn't rebound? Well, the coming chapters are all about that. The three-step success formula helps you in becoming a strong and proactive observer of your reality. The more unidirectional your intentions, attention, emotions, beliefs, and imagination are, the better you will be able to control your life.

Chapter 3
Reinventing Yourself

"The only lies for which we are truly punished are those we tell ourselves."

—V. S. Naipaul (author)

Even when you are the observer, the captain, the master, the chef, the jockey, and the artesian of your life, you still create a reality that is different from that of your dreams! You still might fall ill, meet with an accident, go bankrupt, face a divorce, or get hurt in relationships. But the important point here is that no matter what happens, it's always your own doing. In this world, nobody is somebody else's victim. Each person is a victim of his or her own thoughts.

As you saw in the concluding section of the last chapter, things are not working out for you because you have lost the power of engaging in proactive observation. This is the result of the present limitations of your brain and the conditioning of your subconscious mind. You may read hundreds of books on positive thinking, but if your internal programming is set for negativity, you will keep coming back to square one. Inspiring words are not enough to change your reality. A superficial knowledge of thought-power and its application will be worthless. To draw its benefits to the fullest, it is important to understand the origin of your limiting thoughts. You will have to make substantial changes to your thinking pattern. If I straightaway ask you to be positive and visualise yourself closing a huge business deal, it won't be easy for you. Inevitably, all beliefs pertaining to why that deal can't happen will rush into your imagination. Your thoughts will be ineffective because your mind will continue to nag you that this success image is fake and can't come to fruition. To help the thought-power to work, you need to have focused and consistent thoughts free from doubts. Your thoughts and the beliefs of your subconscious mind should be in sync with your goals.

This chapter will guide you in getting rid of unwanted beliefs to make room for new and optimistic ones which is the third step in the successful application of thought-power. We will see how your thoughts and emotions lead to the subconscious conditioning of your mind, which in turn, affects your beliefs about self and society. You will understand the role of the brain and subconscious mind and then move on to apply this knowledge for changing your thoughts, beliefs, and emotions. This section is a must-read for those of you who have been applying thought-power with little or no success. You may ask for anything from the energy of the universe, but you will not be able to do much about it until your mind believes it and thinks that it is possible.

Understanding your framework (Old Beliefs)

↓

Remoulding your framework (New Beliefs)

Figure: Reinventing yourself by bringing in a new framework

Let me walk you through the journey of reinventing yourself by becoming an observer who has a mental predisposition for positivity and whose thoughts and emotions are synchronised for creating reality by choice.

Brain

Understanding a tiny bit about your brain will help you make better choices of your thoughts. The human brain is an extremely magnificent creation. It governs all vital body processes. There are about 100 billion nerve cells in the brain called neurons. These neurons have branches that help them communicate with other neurons. All the neurons involved in a particular brain activity come together to form connections which are known as neural networks.

The brain receives 400 billion bits of information per second but we are only aware of about 2000 of those. This is because the brain excludes tremendous data that it considers non-essential. The relevance of information is determined based on previous memories in our subconscious mind and whether a neural network for that information exists. But why are we talking about the brain's ability to perceive information? It is because this suggests that the brain sometimes limits our perception by repeating an old set of patterns and habits. Consequently, as these old sets of thoughts keep on recurring, your old reality also keeps on repeating.

The activities, behaviours, and habits that you perform frequently get established as neural networks in the brain. For instance, if you keep getting angry at the slightest disagreement, you make this a part of your behaviour by developing a neural network for it. The neural network responsible for your anger becomes dominant and whenever any kind of disagreement occurs, these neurons fire up and you burst into anger. When such situations occur repeatedly, you become addicted to the emotion of anger.

This knowledge about the importance of building the right neural patterns in our brain is effective in aiding the creation of right thoughts. You can consciously change your undesirable habits, emotions, and behaviours related to a particular situation and thus also change your thinking pattern for such situations. So, in order to be a proactive thinker, you can employ this concept of the brain's neuroplasticity. As hardwired neural networks form out of repetitive behaviours and habits, they can be broken by changing the habits and associated behaviours. And if you start changing your thinking pattern, old and unwanted neural networks are destroyed through a process called synaptic pruning. This will lead to the emergence of conscious thoughts from your brain rather than the repetition of spontaneous and preprogrammed old thoughts.

Use this biological information to make your thoughts an outcome of choice rather than an automatic, default response. More positive thoughts and emotions will aid the development of more desirable neural networks that will help you respond similarly in other situations. Take the leap towards changing your thoughts and habits. Remember that all the thoughts that have emerged from your brain until now have culminated into what you have become today.

Subconscious Mind

"Whatever we plant in our subconscious mind and nourish with repetition and emotion will one day become a reality."

—Earl Nightingale (author)

Unlike the brain, which is a tangible organ that controls the functions of other organs, the mind is the invisible part that is associated with beliefs, thoughts, memories, and imagination. The subconscious mind is said to be the inner or subjective mind, while the conscious mind is the outer or objective mind. The conscious mind performs logical and conscious actions that are not automatic responses and involve some thinking, judgement, or analysis. For instance, you use your conscious mind while performing calculations, whereas driving the car and simultaneously listening to music is a subconscious activity.

The subconscious mind is the non-judgemental mind that believes in everything you feed into it. It is the storehouse of your skills, knowledge, experiences, and memories. Do you remember playing with block puzzles as a child? Whenever you wished to connect the blocks to complete the puzzle, you picked out pieces from the box and then joined them to complete the puzzle. The information stored in the subconscious mind can be compared to all the blocks of a puzzle which are kept together in a box. Whenever the situation demands, the information is retrieved from the mind's storehouse.

Also, we know now that thoughts are generated by a complex cascade of processes in which the act of thinking is determined by neurons (brain cells). The subconscious mind is the source of the information that generates thought. This information can be in the form of an idea, image, memory, vision, awareness, experience, or belief. Thus, conscious actions and thoughts are based on what you already know and all your desires and creativity take birth from the subconscious mind. In fact, the subconscious mind is the non-physical identity that governs all that is happening in your physical world! It is like the raw material that the architect uses to construct a house. According to the quality and quantity of the raw material used, different designs emerge. Similarly, the types of thoughts that emerge depend on the information stored in the subconscious mind.

Now, you have to decide what type of information you want to feed into your subconscious mind. But remember that each time this information will be retrieved from the database to create your thoughts. So, if you take up positivity, you will nurture your mind with this positive soil and in return, it will give you sweet results in the form of free-flowing positive thoughts.

To know more about the role of your subconscious mind in defining your day to day life, *The Power of Your Subconscious Mind* by Dr Joseph Murphy is a good read. And if you want to gain a scientific perspective of how your environment and your beliefs are shaping your reality, *The Biology of Belief* by Dr Bruce Lipton will broaden your knowledge.

Attuning the Subconscious Mind

> *"Know that you can remake yourself by giving a new blueprint to your subconscious mind."*
>
> —Dr Joseph Murphy (author)

According to biologist Dr Bruce Lipton, in a day, we use our conscious mind only 5% of the times. The remaining 95% of the times, our thoughts, decisions, and actions are based on the pre-existing data stored in the subconscious mind. He further clarifies that the programming of a child's mind begins before birth in the mother's womb. Between the ages 2 and 6 years, the child's brain generates theta waves, which pertain to 'downloading' all sorts of information into the subconscious mind like a hypnosis session. The conscious brain is still inactive, and thus the child takes up all information without analysing or filtering it. The child also internalises the 'rules of living' from the parents and society. Therefore, it becomes essential to keep a check on what has been fed in your mind in the past and what you are feeding into it now. Do not let your 6-year-old self create your life today.

So, you see, everything you perceive through your senses is recorded in the subconscious mind and these records are retrieved whenever needed. Until now, you have been recording most of the data unconsciously. The crucial thing to understand is that we are living in a world wherein you will keep encountering a lot of negative energy from people and experiences. However, being aware and proactive can help you stop such negativity at the gate and avoid their retention in your mind's storehouse. To become a proactive thinker, you have to be a conscious receiver of information. And if you do not make conscious efforts to change what is being fed to your mind, it will take upon whatever it perceives on a daily basis.

Once you become aware of the importance of certain information that your mind should absorb (ideas, images, memories, experiences, beliefs, etc.), the next step is to attune your subconscious mind to harmonise it with the reality you want to create. For this, you have to decide your aim and register it in your subconscious mind. Your mind will then create corresponding thoughts and search its database to identify options that can bring you closer to the achievement of your goal.

Few key facts associated with the subconscious mind which can be tapped into to think proactively have been shared below. These will help you to deliberately shift your thinking patterns in the required direction once you start following the three-step success formula which has been mentioned later.

❖ **Power of Repetition**

Fascinating neuroscience research reveals that our brains have an internal system of clearing out the unused data stored in it. During a biological process called synaptic pruning, less-used neural networks are marked up for degradation by the glial cells of the brain. This way, negative thoughts associated with a bad experience can be erased by ignoring these thoughts for a few days. The opposite also happens, i.e. repetitive thoughts and actions strengthen the corresponding neural connections. This suggests that you can focus on building more neural connections that lead to positive thoughts and outcomes. So, instead of recalling a brawl you got into with somebody on the street while driving, try recalling a Saturday night dinner date with your partner.

At first it seems difficult, but you can develop a habit of thinking optimistically. By using these 3 tips:

1. Have a 'STOP' signal that you can evoke whenever a negative thought emerges. Say 'stop' and replace the thought by saying some positive word or phrase like 'I am joyful'.
2. Secondly, whenever you are unable to stop your negative mental chatter, close your eyes and take deep breaths. As you keep doing this, negative thoughts will start fading away. Soon you will find that such thoughts knock at your doorstep less

frequently as if they know that this is a no-entry zone for them.

3. Thirdly you can make use of distraction. When something is bothering you continuously, distract yourself by doing something different. This can include calling a friend, watching a comedy clip, engaging yourself with some household work, playing with kids, reading a book, etc.

❖ Inability to Differentiate between Reality and Imagination

Research has shown that the electrical activity that occurs in the brain is the same when a person is experiencing a real situation and when he or she creates it in the mind via imagination. In their study on mental imagery, Marc Jeannerod and Jean Decety wrote, "The mapping of brain activity during motor imagery discloses a pattern of activation similar to that of an executed action." This means that the same set of neurons fire in the brain whether you actually experience reality or imagine it.

Then, why not harness this non-judgemental feature of the subconscious mind by visualising your goals and targets. Be an active participant in designing your life rather than passively waiting for the mind to react. This concept of using thoughts for creative visualisation is known as Visual-Motor Rehearsal which has been discussed in detail in Chapter 6.

❖ Brain Filters

The Reticular Activating System or RAS is a complex network of nerve pathways in the brain stem connecting the spinal cord with parts of forebrain and hindbrain. Together with other biochemical pathways, the RAS acts as a brain filter for the massive amount of information that is received by the brain. It helps the brain become consciously alert to receive sensory information. For example, as you read this book, there are many sounds and objects in the background, but the RAS helps the brain ignore this irrelevant background information.

But how does the brain determine the relevance of the information that it is being bombarded with? This depends on what is stored in your subconscious mind (knowledge, interests, beliefs, ideas, etc.) and what prevails in your dominant thoughts. Subjects that you focus on more are given precedence as relevant data to process. So, when you start thinking proactively towards your goals, more often the RAS will take in information that is relevant to your goals. With practise, this proactive observer approach will guide the RAS to look for ideas and opportunities that are apt for your growth. By deliberately paying attention to positive and required information, you will be able to create the desired filter for your brain.

Beliefs: Your Portrait of the World

> *"Your chances of success in any undertaking can always be measured by your belief in yourself."*
>
> —Robert Collier (author)

On an average, your brain can generate up to 50,000 thoughts per day. Out of these, 95% are the ones that are repeated daily. This repetition of thoughts leads to their assimilation in your subconscious mind and compromises most of your beliefs. A thought is powerless until you make it a belief and accept it to be true. Once they turn into beliefs, these thoughts assume a comfortable and permanent position in your mind, until they are replaced by new beliefs.

Repetitive thoughts become BELIEFS

↓

Beliefs get ingrained in the SUBCONSCIOUS MIND

↓

The BRAIN thinks THOUGHTS that satisfy its beliefs

↓

EMOTIONS get linked to the thoughts

↓

You perform ACTIONS

↓

Actions result in HABITS

↓

Habits determine REALITY

Figure: Role of beliefs in creating your reality

Beliefs are stored in your subconscious mind as a collection of facts, ideas, and knowledge that have convinced you about your image of reality. Even when you start on a journey of positive thinking, if your underlying belief is that you cannot succeed, no amount of positive thoughts can help you. Only thoughts that have been crystallised into beliefs can manifest. The observer can only give his or her undivided focus to a thought he or she has complete belief in. Whether you pray that you are blessed with riches or you are afraid of being broke, you will achieve only what matches your beliefs because each time you think, talk, write, observe, visualise, complain, grumble, fret, etc., your beliefs come into play.

The next thing to consider is that why do you keep recreating the same situations in your lives when it comes to job, money, love, etc.? There are so many other options available, but you overlook them. This is because the mind becomes conditioned to understanding and believing only some set patterns of beliefs. With time you get so hypnotised by your pre-existing beliefs that you forget to make any effort to shred them. You can become conscious of your beliefs by paying attention to your repetitive thoughts. Being aware and selective about what you are thinking helps you develop better beliefs which lead to better choices, and finally, to better results.

A wonderful example of subconscious beliefs can be seen in the taming of a baby elephant. The baby elephant's leg is tied to a pole using a strong rope or chain so that it does not wander away. In spite of all the pulling, the baby elephant is unable to walk away. Now when this baby elephant grows up into a 12-feet-tall giant, tying it to a pole will be of no help as it can easily break away from the rope together with the pole! But actually, tying the elephant to a pole is no longer needed. Trainers merely tie a rope around the legs and the elephant is left loose. However, by now, the subconscious mind of the elephant has been programmed that while the rope is around its legs it cannot go anywhere. Thus, an animal as huge as an elephant gets tamed to not wander away.

Many of you too have bounded yourself to some self-sabotaging chains which are easy to break if you pay attention. You cannot be successful at applying thought-power until you have complete faith in what you are thinking. Thought-power will always hold true. If you find that it is not working for you, then you have to analyse your beliefs. Proactive thinking works, but only to the extent of the beliefs that you hold about the accomplishment of your goals. Whether you will achieve something that you focus your intentions on is contingent on what you believe about it. Therefore, it is very beneficial to understand your beliefs about money, love, career etc., before consciously applying thought-power. Your intentions as an observer should carry some substance with it; it cannot be some vague or fake desires and daydreams.

In Chapter 2, we talked about the placebo effect. It is a great example of the impact of beliefs on the body. If your mind tells the trillions of cells in your body that they cannot be healed after this injury, what message do you think those tiny cells get? The mind will tailor all the body processes to match your beliefs. This is the way it works.

Similarly, prayers are such beautiful examples of beliefs. When you pray, you have undivided faith that some supreme power will take care of your wishes. This true belief leads to right thoughts, which lead to right actions, and thus to the fulfilment of your goals.

Some Research:

- A famously cited study conducted at Harvard University by A. J. Crum and E. J. Langer proved how our beliefs have remarkable control over our mind. In their study, the staff at a hotel was informed that their daily work provides them with the exercise required to lead a healthy lifestyle. A control group, which was not provided any such information, was also monitored for 1 month. Compared with the control group, the 'informed' group ". . . showed a decrease in weight, blood pressure, body fat, waist-to-hip ratio, and body mass index." This proved that an individual's beliefs and thoughts can greatly impact his or health and body.

- In a review by M. R. Asha et al. (2009), the beliefs are said to be stimuli received as trusted information, and that they are responsible for moral judgement, decision-making, the emergence of psychopathology symptoms, cognitive and emotional assessments, addiction, and persistent normal defensive reactions.

- In a 2013 research on using the placebo effect to enhance cognitive performance of the mind, psychologists and researchers U. W. Eger and S. Loughnan wrote, "People have significant psychological resources to improve their well-being and performance, but these resources often go unused and could be better harnessed."

Your thoughts may not be the truth; rather, they present various versions of the truth which you believe subconsciously. If you intend to change your thinking pattern, you have to change what is already present in your mind. You have to clean the slate first before you write something new on it. Therefore, it is essential to change the blueprint of your beliefs imprinted on your subconscious mind. For this, the next section deals with identifying the origin of our negative beliefs in order to rectify them.

Source of Your Beliefs

> *"Our beliefs about the world and our systems for functioning in the world are all embedded in us through the flow and progression of culture from the minds of the people around us into our baby brains."*
>
> —Vishen Lakhiani (entrepreneur)

Who tells you what success is, how to earn money, how to look beautiful, why to have a 9 to 5 job, when to get a college degree, why a business is risky, how big your pay cheque should be, what is best for you, what should be on your bucket list, etc.? There are so many whys, hows, and whats in life! You get input in every walk of your life from society, religion, culture, family, teachers, friends, incidents, environment, books, etc. You keep accumulating this information in the form of thoughts, and later as beliefs, throughout your life. But the most significant period when you absorb these beliefs like a sponge is childhood. It is the time when you quickly ingrain these experiences and information into your mind without weighing them consciously.

Your everyday learnings from the people and environment around you are necessary as they form the basis of your survival. But not all that you learn is the truth. Not everything that has been fed into your mind is correct. The conditions in which you were brought up and the experiences that you continue to encounter leave a strong impression on your mind about success.

Beliefs are also perpetuated from one generation to the other in the form of habits, knowledge, and common sense. Childhood indoctrination is inescapable. Since you were born, you have looked up to your parents for guidance, after which came your teachers, mentors, and so on. Their experience, no doubt, is of great help, but they can also limit you from experiencing new ways of life. The person whom you authorise to guide you can share only his or her beliefs with you.

Let's take these examples of how childhood conversations and experiences with the family can result in a deep-rooted self-esteem belief in a person.

- Do you remember a time when your child came running to you, all excited, to show you a star which he got for his homework? Instead of appreciating him, your response was, "For the next time, I want you to earn 3 stars like your friend Avi."
- One day, your child was trying to wear her school shoes all by herself. When she was ready, you found that she had interchanged the pair. Frustrated with the morning chores, you shout at her that she could not wear her shoes correctly despite having seen how you do it when you make her wear the shoes.

If such episodes keep on repeating then what do you think these two behaviours will do to your kid's self-esteem? He or she, too young to understand anything, will believe in their meaning-making mind, which will tell them 'I am not as worthy as my friend' or 'I can't do stuff correctly'. There are many such incidences where disarray is created in the kid's mind, disrupting their ego, confidence, loyalty, compassion, kindness, calmness, sincerity, and self-control.

Being a mother, I understand that dealing with kids can be a tough task, especially when you also have office work or daily chores to complete. But try not to make your kids that innocent box where you can dump all your day's frustrations and grudges.

Parents, too busy with their laptops and iPhones, are unaware of the fact that they might unconsciously instil in their child the belief that they do not deserve enough attention. With time, you forget such events or experiences. But the repercussions they leave on your and your child's mind remain in the form of a belief until it is overtaken by some other belief.

Most of the time, you don't even know why a particular hampering belief developed or why you continue to have a negative reaction to a particular situation. Incorporating beliefs is an unconscious process generally. Gradually, these erroneous and untrue beliefs start ruling your life. Guidance from society and family is very important for the overall personality development of an individual, but many a time, this guidance transforms into rules, which no one is allowed to break. You get imprisoned in that narrow thinking and stop pursuing your dreams. Basically, when the seeds themselves are inviable, how do you expect a flower to blossom?

As you grow up, you start questioning some beliefs and the rest you keep absorbing. Sometimes you know that what you have been told by others is not true, but you are not sure if you can or should challenge that idea because you do not want to be an outcast. The need for belonging makes you accept these unwanted beliefs easily and so you buy and sell yourself the opinions of others. In his book, *The Four Agreements,* Don Miguel Ruiz quotes, "The fear of being rejected becomes the fear of not being good enough.

Eventually we become someone that we are not. We become a copy of mamma's beliefs, daddy's beliefs, society's beliefs and religion's beliefs."

Absolute Truth and Relative Truth

"Choose beliefs that serve your soul—choose beliefs that serve the grander dream of who you choose to be."

—Joy Page (actress)

Before you make a decision, have a look as to what is responsible for your decision—is it a relative truth or an absolute truth? Is it universal or man-made belief? You have to decide if your goals are really yours, or have they been imposed on you as a rule to live by. Also, you have to see if there exist any different and worthy ways of achieving your goals instead of following some rigid and outdated path to success defined by other fellow human beings.

Most of the time, you will come across people who will tell you why it is impossible to achieve your dreams and ambitions. They will tell you about all the obstacles and barriers that lie on the path to your success and will rarely say, "Yeah you can do it! Go for it." Did you ever think why people do this? This is because it is easy to be negative. It is easy to take shortcuts, promote negative beliefs, feel jealous, loose temper, and get impatient. But it takes effort to be calm and supportive. Evolution had programmed our brains to avoid risk and play safe. Even though today we do not have to save ourselves from tigers hidden in the woods, but this primitive brain of ours is still scared of any life situation that appears to be insecure and difficult. On the other hand, happiness is a tough and strong emotion. Let me explain this. So, try complaining, grudging, and talking negatively about something or someone for 5 minutes. Now, try standup comedy for 5 minutes. Which one is more difficult to do?

Let's consider the role of beliefs with these examples:

- Yash comes from a financially compromised background. His deep-seated fear of not having enough money leads him to drop the idea of starting his own marketing firm. If only Yash could have the courage to explore a variety of financial help options available nowadays, he could move towards fulfilling his ambitions.
- Sana has a family history of diabetes. The stress and fear arising from knowing the fact that diabetes can often be hereditary may lead Sana to be an easy prey for the disease (nocebo effect). Today, thanks to studies in the area of epigenetics, scientists are able to prove that an individual has an enormous amount of control on the expression of his or her genes. By changing their thoughts and environmental signals, one can control their genetic traits. So, by feeding your mind with the right thoughts and your body with the right food and environment, one can reverse the process of physical and emotional ill-being.
- Sometimes in life, we come across people who are quadriplegic or have dysfunctional limbs because of some disease, but they are able to do things like any other human being. They can write, paint, walk, and partake in many kinds of regular and creative endeavours. This is because they have surpassed the beliefs related to what medical science told them and

are trying to move ahead with a new belief by making their other organs work for them. We come across several stories of Guinness World Records where a person is able to pull an airplane or a heavy vehicle like a truck with their little finger or moustache. How do you think they achieve these extraordinary feats? Of course, by practise. But they achieved these feats also by training their mind differently than the majority of people. They have talked their brain into believing that their muscles are capable of lifting or pulling that heavy weight.

The negative thoughts emerging from impeding beliefs become self-harming energy blocks that stop you from living your dreams. The variety of fears you hold inside you—regarding public speaking, launching your own business, asking for a promotion, pursuing your underlying aspirations, travelling across the world, asking that girl out, writing a book, picking up a musical instrument, joining a sports club, etc.—originate because your dominant thoughts are 'It's too hard to get', 'I don't deserve it', 'It is too big a decision', 'I don't have enough money', 'It's too late', etc. So, it is important to be cautious of what you speak. Words impress themselves in your mind and come out as thoughts. Negative self-talk keeps strengthening your beliefs by the repetitive thoughts it accompanies. What you tell yourself about your personality and experiences, your mind considers it to be true. There forms a negativity loop, where your thoughts lead to beliefs, which lead to negative self-talk, which in turn strengthens your beliefs. Do not try to find solace in speaking about your faults, shortcomings, or failures. When you don't want them, why talk about them!

The self-imposed boundaries, in the form of beliefs, lead to procrastination, criticising the situation, blaming others for your failures, losing temper, hopelessness, low self-esteem, fear, increased stress, etc. which then turns into physical pain and several other negative experiences. You become so used to a set pattern of thinking that if there is something out of the box, you try to squash it to the point that it fits into the box (mind), even if it ends up distorting the box.

Mentioned below are a few common areas where you generally tend to form a false viewpoint. These are some of the many myths you have taken over during your upbringing or from self-experiences.

❖ **Love**

In this category, some of the prominent myths include true love doesn't exist, I am not beautiful enough, love always leads to heartbreaks, I will never find my soulmate, looks are important if you want a good partner, etc.

❖ **Career**

When it comes to career, some of the common myths include I can't qualify in the interview because I am not experienced enough, there are not enough vacancies, there is too much competition out there, my passion and job can't be the same, my degree will not fetch me a good job, I don't have enough resources to learn that new skill, I don't deserve that job, I do not have enough support to pass the examination, I belong to a lower/middle-class background and so the world is tough for me, I can't fulfil my parent's expectations, my IQ is not high enough to get good grades, my personality ruins my interviews, etc.

❖ **Health**

Some of the prominent myths in this category include the disease runs in my family, my illness is permanent, I can't recover from my ill health, etc.

❖ **Wealth**

In this category, some of the prominent myths include wealthy people inherit their money, their wealth is more out of luck than from a long haul, best education opportunities made them rich, one can get rich only by employing wrong ways of earning money, I am financially incapable to start a business, I don't earn enough, I can't afford that car, money does not come easily, I am always in debt, money is not important, etc. Interestingly, countering these prominent money-beliefs, research suggests that 70-80% of the rich are self-made millionaires. Their parents did not leave them an empire. It was their continuous focus and passion that helped them achieve their goals.

These misapprehensions about abundance, love, health, and success have made your mind a confined space. These beliefs are relative truths and not absolute. They assure you and remind you of the inabilities which don't exist in the real world. And until you clean your mind from these faulty beliefs, all your desperate attempts to succeed will land up in the trash bin. Once you fall victim to them, you will attract more such thoughts, people, and situations, which will further dishearten you.

After contemplating on the above section, you can try out an exercise for yourself given below:

Categorise your life into the following sections: love life, family relationships, parenting, intellectual life, social life, health, education, finances, career, personality, quality of life, and spiritual life. Under each section, write down the impeding beliefs that have been holding you back in excelling in that part of your life. Next, write down a new self-aiding belief you can form to overcome that limiting belief. This analysis will help you in forming your affirmations and action plans for wholesome growth.

Building an Unhampered Belief System

"Be fearless in the pursuit of what sets your soul on fire."

—Jennifer Lee (screenwriter)

It is said that when Napoleon Bonaparte was a child, he was given a red sapphire and was asked to take care of it because the owner of that sapphire will become the emperor of France. This prophecy resulted in an undying belief in Napoleon about his potential for being an emperor—and as we all know, the prophecy turned out to be true. Was that sapphire supernatural? No, but the thoughts its possession generated carried the power to change Napoleon's destiny.

Do not let uninvited experiences from the past exploit your thought-power. Until you change the cassette (beliefs), the tape recorder (mind) will keep playing the same songs (thoughts). Remember how, as a child, you were stubborn about getting a candy. But as you grew up, you started compromising. This habit affects every facet of our lives

This time, make a list of goals without underestimating the power of your thoughts. When your thoughts will be powerful like a strong tree with its root penetrating deep into your mind, storms of pessimistic perception will not last for long.

Change your BELIEFS

↓

GOALS and beliefs are aligned

↓

THOUGHTS become goal-oriented

↓

Desired REALITY is created

Figure: New beliefs result in new reality

You have to shatter the ropes that are strangling you and stopping you to breathe freely in the air of hope and positivity. In a step-by-step manner, release all the unwanted energy residing in your mind. When you open your mind to a fresh perspective, you will notice possibilities lined up at your doorstep. If somebody tells you, "This isn't possible," then run away in the opposite direction and find a different possibility.

Often, you discuss your goals with your family and friends, but the results don't show up because, more or less, you keep living the same behaviours that hinder the change you want. The three-step success formula mentioned in the next chapter will give you handy ways of utilising thought-power by becoming a proactive observer and thinker. But before you move on to that, it is important to wash away your myths about success and happiness. To fit in some new positivity, you will have to clean your mind's slate. So, let's spend some time to unlearn all the misconceptions you have downloaded in your subconscious mind since childhood. Focusing on something without actually believing in it is a sheer waste of time as this way, your affirmations and visualisations will go against your goals.

As a social animal, each day you live with faith, whether it's faith in a supreme power, in your family, in the government, etc. This helps you survive. But if you start living with faith in yourself, you will not just survive but live life to the grandest. Supportive beliefs are the backbones of thoughts that are nourishing for the soul.

Few ways that will help you develop beliefs to nurture your goals are listed below:

❖ **Understanding the Roots of Your Belief**

When you identify your doubts, guilt, lack, fear, anger, resentment, frustration, or any negative emotion that is holding you back, run a backward loop to identify the bottom cause. For instance, some past trauma, family crisis, unfulfilled goals, lack of education, betrayal, loss of love, etc., can lead to negative thoughts that harbour your subconscious mind. Every time you encounter any one of these situations, without conscious consideration, your mind will trigger similar thoughts and emotions. Identify if your fears and doubts are due to your internal beliefs or external circumstances. Once you identify and reshape a negative belief, you can generate desired thoughts and an undivided faith that it is possible to achieve those goals. This new-found confidence will supercharge you.

At any point in time, if you are aware of your misleading beliefs, you can choose to believe in something new about yourself. You can always choose a more empowering belief than the one you believed in minutes before. Initially, the brain tries to talk you out of any new belief that you try to feed it. Efforts will be needed to pull out that fear- and guilt-laden baby you are hiding inside of you. Every day, give yourself the permission to live a better life than the previous day. The past is always an old version of you. But today, you have the choice to make a better you . . . a new you. Each day, you are reborn to hundreds of new prospects and ideas of living a personified life.

❖ Stop Being Judgemental

Do you judge what a female should do in society? Do you judge what your role should be in your current job? If so, you are imposing a limit in the form of your opinions. Unwanted opinions should neither be given nor accepted. Do not be a part of discussions that are judgemental about something or someone. Give yourself and others an opportunity to grow and thrive in this world.

This is one of the most important things you can do to change your belief system. Open yourself to new knowledge, new people, new cultures, and new ways of doing things. When you start to think that your current knowledge is the only way out, you automatically ignore all the other easy or beneficial paths that can help you. Respect the disparities and possibilities that exist in this world. A flexible mind with a growth mindset will have beliefs that will focus on achievements.

❖ Think with a Free Mind

Stop telling yourself things like "This can't be done", "This always happens to me", "Life won't spare me", "It is too tough for me", "I have inherited it from my family", and so on. Instead of saying, "That's the way it is", find ways to explore what it can be. These compromises will keep adding frustration and challenges in all dimensions of your life.

Consider this scenario. Dhruv and Ali are two friends from an economically fragile background. Both have big dreams of owning a self-started business. Dhruv is surrounded by a bubble of negative beliefs, which keep on whispering to him, "People like him with a simple graduation degree and hardly any money to survive should not poke their nose into dreams which belong only to the rich." Dhruv's standpoint regarding money, poverty, education, and earnings are so pessimistic that even when Ali tells him that by having a positive approach and taking right decisions one by one, they can set up their own business, Dhruv is unable to rectify his faulty beliefs. Ten years down the line, Ali is the owner of well-doing textile trading firm and Dhruv is doing 2-3 part-time jobs per day to clear his bills.

In *Rich Dad Poor Dad*, a book that truly inspired me to think out-of-the-box, author Robert Kiyosaki gives an eye-opening description of prevalent beliefs about money in our society. He writes, "'I can't afford it', shuts down your brain. 'How can I afford it?' opens up possibilities, excitement and dreams." By focusing on abundance, you can collapse all the negative possibilities of lack.

Often, we limit our potential by comparing ourselves with others. It is common to have such self-talk:

- "When my elder brother has failed in the business, then how can I bring fortune to it?" Here, you think that you are less than your brother since he is more experienced than you.

- "Sia is vacationing in Greece as she has a wealthy husband." Here, you unconsciously make a wealth-boundary in your mind that you can never be rich enough for a vacation abroad.

This comparison with others on the basis of well-being, family background, intelligence, etc. should maintain a healthy borderline that inspires you to do more. People who have achieved what you desire should be looked upon as role models or simply as a source of inspiration. They should not become a roadblock to stumble upon and fall. Everyone is made up of the same stuff—energy. The difference lies not in your fundamental constitution but in your mind. Comparing yourself to others dulls your sparkle. Shine in your own vibrant way.

❖ Have an Optimistic Approach

You cannot stop every event from occurring because you are not the reason behind all of them. But surely, you can choose what to interpret and feed into your mind from a particular event. If you are too eager to derive meaning out of an experience, then choose the right belief. Condition the mind to perceive the positives.

For instance, if you grew up in a household where your parents did not get along well with each other, there are two ways of interpreting this scenario so as to instil a belief in your mind. From what you have experienced, your opinion about marriages can be "Relationships and marriages are worthless, and I will never fall for anything like this" or it can be "I will learn from my parent's mistake and will make a wonderful spouse as not all marriages end up in such turmoil". Now, in which case do you think you will end up with a happy married life?

Do not be an unnecessary critic watching depressing news of war, accidents, theft, etc. Either you should build the capability to free the world of its problems or else stop discussing them and empowering them with your constant energy. This way, you are only feeding your mind with negative thoughts like "How gloom-ridden the world is!" Unconsciously, you are catching up with the belief that this world is full of so many obstructions that it will never be easy for you to survive here.

❖ Rise above the Fear of Standing Alone

"What will people say?" is one of the biggest fears of people world over. So many of you keep following your ordinary, purposeless life just because of the fear of criticism. The belief that your ambitious actions towards your goals will raise many eyebrows has ripped off your wings. Till the time you are not harming anyone in the process of your growth, you are free to move on.

If you believe that you are not worthy for that promotion, then guess what? You will never stand up for yourself and ask for it. Since you never let the boss know about your efforts towards accomplishing company's visions, how can you expect to be promoted? Tear apart the fabric of illusion and stand up for the reality that you think you deserve.

Today is the time when you can make a change happen. Else, when you will grow old and are lying on your deathbed, remember that you will regret not standing up for yourself. Let this not happen. Let your inner self guide you so that you can shine in this world. Dream big with an open mind. Only you can decide your true worth. Do not judge yourself with someone else's lens. Once you gather the courage to be true to yourself, you will be unstoppable. Create your day your way. Start acting to reshape your life, instead of reacting to what life offers.

❖ Realising Abundance

The energy of the universe is not some disaster-management team with limited stocks of food and money. No one will ever have the scarcity of joy just because some other person has asked for more of it from the universe. Since thinking is in your hands, no one other than you can decide how much abundance you deserve in your life. Universal energy is in abundance for everyone—it wants you to be bountiful. Don't be afraid that by the time you end up with your degree, your course will not be of any value, or that by the time you will be free to take a Christmas break, all good travel deals will end. There are lots of vibrant possibilities in each direction.

The true nature of life is free-flowing advancement, content, and bliss. There is nothing wrong in aspiring for great things in life. It is not selfish if you want to earn some more money, go on a vacation, buy a large car, or have a comfortable lifestyle. Till the time your desires are in harmony with nature, there is nothing to be doubtful about. It's a win-win game for all. There is no need for unjust competition, jealousy, greed, betrayal, or blame game.

❖ Keep Away from the Belief 'My Destiny Is Fixed'

Destiny is a blockage that either you or the society has imposed upon you. It is not responsible for your sickness or poverty. Only when you do not take things under your control, you blame destiny. That's a victim-mentality. Destiny lies within your control because your thoughts are under your control. It is not prewritten; rather, it is written every day by you as you go through the cycle of thoughts each day. All the experiences in your life are the result of your own thinking pattern and thus blaming others is futile. At the end of the day, it is you who is living in turmoil by blaming others.

Why do you think that you encounter compromises and struggles? Just because you were born so? No. Even if you come from an economically weak family, you are unique. You are not what your family is. As Bill Gates once said, "If you are born poor, it's not your mistake. But if you die poor, it's your mistake."

In personal psychology, 'locus of control' is a belief about the degree of control one has over his or her life as opposed to external forces and events beyond their control. Expanding your locus of control helps you in moving out of the victim-mentality. From self-devastation to self-creation, start the journey. Whatever are your inner desires, bring them forward from the back of your mind and don't let them suffocate and die. You are an observer—think and create! You are life and life is for you, not against you.

After understanding the connection between your beliefs and thoughts and how pivotal it is in creating your day, let us see the role of your emotions in fueling your thoughts and hence, your life.

Thoughts and Emotions

"Be happy for this moment. This moment is your life."
—Omar Khayyam (philosopher)

By now, you know that conscious thinking is pivotal for leading a fulfilling life. Controlling all the 50,000 thoughts per day is impossible, but since 95% of them are repetitive, the task becomes feasible. Your emotions play an important part here. Emotions are biochemical responses that your brain generates during various experiences and feelings are your reaction to a particular emotion. A similar situation can arouse different feelings in different individuals. Out of the total of 34,000 emotions, we experience only 10 to 12 daily!

Identifying what thoughts are running in your mind at a particular time is difficult than identifying the associated feeling it generates. Authors Esther and Jerry Hicks call this 'The Emotional Guidance System'. By having a close guard on your feelings, you can have a close watch over your thoughts. And this is extremely important if you want to embark upon a journey of self-correction.

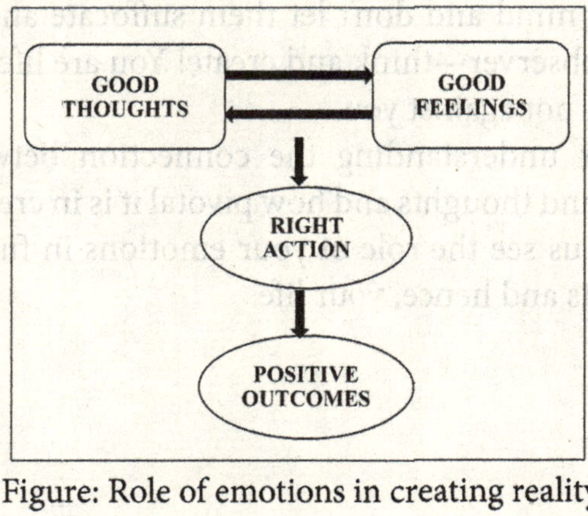

Figure: Role of emotions in creating reality

If you are feeling low, you can trace back to identify the belief or thought behind that feeling. This way, you can have control over the pessimistic thoughts running in your mind. If you are grief-stricken because you don't have sufficient resources for your kid's education, you will have to stop here to change your thoughts. Thoughts of 'lack' can never attract abundance in your or your child's life.

Mind your feelings throughout the day. Do not let the daily routine or circumstances spoil your mood and make you feel angry or irritated. Maintain a calm and composed disposition. When a thought becomes associated with an emotion, it becomes easy for the mind to download it as a belief. Therefore, what emotions we are attaching to our experiences becomes a topic of significant consideration. You attract everything that you love and hate, or trust and fear.

Childhood abuse, financial crisis in the family, chronic or serious health ailment of a loved one, low self-esteem, unhealthy relationship between parents, etc. are few of the many unwanted experiences that emotionalise your thoughts to the extent that negative thinking sets in as a habit. Unconsciously, you become a person who is always gloomy, mournful, boring, angry, depressed, and regretful. Whenever you notice that a particular bad feeling is becoming associated with your personality, it's time to rewind the cassette and find out the cause.

If you learn to keep track of your emotions and use them to guide your thinking and behaviour, you will master a much-needed psychological trait for leading a successful life—Emotional Intelligence (EQ). Good feelings make you take inspired actions, which, in turn, result in good thoughts. Once your feelings and thoughts are synchronised with your goals, you become unstoppable. By paying attention to your feelings, you can be in the right energy zone. Use your will to adjust your focus. For controlling any unwanted emotions, you can use the same three ways used for stopping negative thoughts. (Discussed above, under the section 'The Power of Repetition')

Some more tips to help you achieve a happy emotional state are as follows:

- Start ignoring negative situations and events around you.
- Try to avoid people who are pessimistic in their approach towards life.
- Be friends with people who share your goals.
- Associate with people who already have what you desire for.
- Identify your passion.
- Nurture a positive habit like gardening, playing a musical instrument, painting, etc.
- Read inspiring articles and books and listen to inspiring videos.
- Watch good stuff on television/Internet which makes you really happy.
- Spend time with kids.
- Take a walk in nature.
- Meditate daily for a few minutes.
- Spend time alone for analysing your daily action plan and long-term goals.
- Appreciate others whenever possible.
- Pay gratitude for all the good things in your life.
- Practise forgiveness.
- Help someone selflessly.

Feelings of love, joy, pleasure, satisfaction, abundance, fulfilment, gratitude, and kindness will tune you in the same frequency as your desired intentions. This will speed up the manifestation process. So, think wisely and guide your emotions. It is never too late to make a difference in your life. It is never too late to be happy again.

Some Research:

According to the Broaden and Build Theory of Positive Emotions enunciated by psychologist B. L. Fredrickson, positive emotions are not just limited to bringing a smile on your face. The 'broaden and build' concept says that positive emotions increase one's awareness, thoughts, actions, resources, and other positive emotions. In her landmark paper of 2004, Dr Fredrickson concluded that:

- Positive emotions broaden thought-action repertoires.
- Positive emotions undo lingering negative emotions.
- Positive emotions fuel psychological resiliency.
- Positive emotions build personal resources.
- Positive emotions fuel psychological and physical well-being.

In Hindu mythology, there are stories about *Kalpvriksha*, the wish-fulfilling tree. The tree had the power of granting the wishes of people. As you gain this new knowledge about your mind, let it become the *Kalpvriksha* of your life.

Now, let us move to the final step of reshaping your thinking pattern—the three-step success formula.

Chapter 4
Unleashing the Power of Your Thoughts

"The essence of magic boils down to the application of two ordinary mental skills: attention and intention. The strength of the magical outcome is modulated by four factors: belief, imagination, emotion, and clarity."

—Dean Radin (scientist)

It may sound clichéd, but it is true that each of the inventions around us were once just a thought in the mind of a dreamer. When you look around, everything you see in your physical world is the manifestation of some idea, which expressed itself as a physical object through a series of transformations. Today, we have the technology to explore outer space, treat deadly diseases, travel in the air, and connect with friends or family who live a thousand miles away. These inventions which have impacted our lives were born out of the thoughts of their inventors. Their vision and imagination preceded reality.

The Three-Step Success Formula

After accepting the power of your thoughts and the science and philosophy behind it, the question that arises is how can you use it proactively all the time? For this, the practitioners of thought-power use a potent three-step success formula (ABR process) to attract abundance in their lives. The three steps, when followed religiously, help you streamline your thoughts to cater to your needs. I am quite excited to share this beautiful, life-changing information with you! The success mantra to attract all the riches and abundance you long for is as follows:

- **Ask (A)** with an open mind

  Asking is the process of *choosing* from the various possible energy waves, which can be collapsed into reality.

- **Believe (B)** in yourself

  Believing helps you *design* and *craft* your choice through imagination.

- **Receive (R)** by performing actions

  Receiving helps you *take action* to speed up the creation of your choice.

The ABR process helps you become a proactive observer. It allows you to deliberately create your reality. Asking and believing are the steps where you send out the thoughts, and receiving is the step where you allow your goals to manifest into reality.

Points to Remember

These steps of creation are extremely powerful. They are the keys to becoming a 'thought-magnet'. If used wisely, they will unlock all the bliss and captivating moments that the universe has in store for you. The pace to accomplish your goals depends on the level of dedication with which you have asked for it and believed in receiving it. The process of creation is delayed if the thoughts are swayed easily. If you hold on to your thoughts strongly, you will notice that the required changes in your life have begun. Don't be reluctant. It's your life and you shouldn't waste your time as those seconds and minutes will turn into years in no time. Few things to keep in mind before we start:

- **It Is Fun, Not Work**

  Each section has practise tips to make the ABR process effective. You should do it with a positive attitude. If you will consider it as a work, it will become burdensome. Focus on the goal instead of the tips. Infuse joy into the ABR process. If you follow it as a homework, you will manifest burdens and not goals!

- **Invincible Faith in Thought-Power**

  Thought-power works, whether you respect its capability or not. Once you start the three-step success formula, some common questions will pop up in your mind like "How will it happen?" and "How is this possible?" The thing is that the 'how' part is never your part. You have to keep faith and you will be guided towards the right actions by your subconscious mind and inner voice. Faith in your thoughts, feelings, and capabilities will guide you to your destination. As someone has famously said, "Faith is like a Wi-Fi. It is invisible, but it has the power to connect you to what you need." Many are unable to manifest because they concentrate too much on 'how'. This creates doubts and desperation. A cynical attitude obstructs directional thinking. You will start reacting rather than acting. Half-hearted efforts lead to incomplete actions that will result in incomplete outcomes. For once, eliminate doubts and limitations. Set your intentions, you will find the way as well.

❖ Gradual Shift in Thinking Pattern

If your present life is different from your desired life, do not expect an overnight change. Your mind has the potential, but it also needs practise and time. The shift to a new pattern of thinking will be gradual and you should respect it. Do not allow anxiety, hesitation, or scepticism to become a hindrance. The ABR process will help remove unwanted, deep-rooted beliefs, and it will give you a completely different outlook on life. Gradual and continuous efforts will make you a proactive observer. Every time you take a step forward in proactive thinking, you will notice an upward shift in your life.

❖ Strengthening the Willpower Muscle

If you have been with me until now, this certainly means that you are ready to make a difference in your life. So far, the chapters contained many theoretical facts. From now onwards, as you learn to use directional use of thought-power, a practical application should also start. Whatever you have learnt will be useful only if you have the willpower to apply it in your life. To stay on the right path, you need to have a will of iron and an unshakable determination to be a proactive thinker. Motivation may fade with time; it is self-discipline that keeps you going. Self-discipline is all about doing the right thing at the right time and in the right amount. The fire within you should be strong enough to sustain you through cold winter nights.

When the mind performs a new task, it has a tendency to revert to its old, relaxed form. Therefore, any new process needs a solid 'stickability'—a sustaining power. Initial days will be tough because you will be challenging the mind to do something that it is not in the habit of doing. When the chattering mind wants to surrender to negative thoughts and play the victim, you have to be tough. Your will should be strong enough to have persistent positive thinking habits instead of occasional outbursts when the situation demands it. The ABR process should be your way of life. Your practise goes in vain if you meditate for an hour and complain the rest of the day. Gratitude or faith should not be a temporary behaviour or feeling, but a daily habit. Your thoughts should be steady in a goal-oriented fashion.

Whatever you have been doing until now, shift it, mould it, and redesign it to include the ABR process in your schedule. For fresh results, a new approach is needed. So, stop procrastinating and start today. Each minute spent in doubt and worry takes you a minute away from your dreams. Thus, it's important to be committed and steadily follow the practises.

❖ Start with Baby Steps

When you start creating with the ABR process, set achievable goals. As you have just started following the ABR process, believable goals strengthen your faith. This is advisable because so far you have not experienced the whole process. If you start with something huge and unbelievable, then you may not achieve it and end up losing faith. Start with something small that is easier to manifest according to you. Once you apply the three-step formula to it and attract it, you can easily rely on your thoughts for massive victories.

For example, if your goal is to buy the latest model of Mercedes within two months but currently you can barely afford a second-hand bike, it becomes difficult for you to have the directional thinking towards buying a Mercedes. Your meaning-making mind will mock you. To avoid this, start with baby steps when it comes to what you are asking. Apply the ABR process for simple daily tasks and problems you want to deal with successfully. Like reaching home on time, finding a parking slot, keeping up with your promise of exercising, getting a call from an old friend, making time to take your kids to the park, healing your stomach ache, etc. Build up your reservoir of belief when it comes to the ABR process. Belief becomes stronger if you can satisfy your sceptical self with proof, whereas doubts can sabotage your ABR process.

❖ Be Good, Do Good

The ABR process is for the goodwill of humanity. Always remember that your thoughts and actions carry a specific energy signature. So, if you try to misuse it in any form, then you will attract that malicious energy in your life as well, in some form or the other.

❖ Practise Tips

Practitioners around the world have used different methods to make the ABR process result-oriented. I have added many such practise tips under each step to speed up your manifestation process. Some of them are widely used while others are from my own experience. These practise tips comprise one of the best ways of becoming a proactive-attraction magnet. The strings of the puppet are in your hands . . . make it dance the way you want!

However, don't be overwhelmed by the number of tips shared in each section. Start with following a few of them, if not all. Practise tips are just a staircase to get to the top. It is not the goal in itself. Your energy should match your goals and not the practise process. With time, you will be able to accommodate these practices in your daily schedule.

Remember, the undefeated rule for life is: success is 80% psychology and 20% mechanics. Your beliefs and emotions drive 80% of the factors that are responsible for success. Your actions, plans, and strategies play 20% role in getting you to your goal. Now that you have mapped the terrain, embark on the path of proactive thinking—the conscious utilisation of thought-power on a daily basis. The coming chapters will further rewire the blueprint of your subconscious mind into a favourable, growth-oriented pattern. I recommend spending sufficient time to contemplate on what you will study in the next three chapters.

Your future awaits you . . . go and give it a tight hug.

Chapter 5

'Ask' With An Open Mind

"Ask, and it will be given to you; seek, and you will find; knock, and it will be opened to you."

—Matthew 7:7, ESV

The energy of the universe is a fountain of surplus happiness, love, wisdom, wealth, health, fame, prosperity, and all that we humans wish for. Asking is about goal-setting and it is the first step for getting things done. The enormous potential of your thoughts is put to action once you decide what to think. It gives glimpses of what will manifest if you follow the creation process.

As an observer, by asking, you define your expectations. Without deciding what your destination is, how would you know which path to take? Without deciding what your intention is, how would you communicate it through your thoughts?

Approach towards Effective Asking

Your thought, intention, attention, and feeling are constituents of thought-power. You have to put your 'feeling' into the asking process. Mere writing or speaking emotionlessly does not work. The practise tips mentioned below will enhance your experience of asking effectively.

❖ Identify Your Goals

Your goals can be something you are passionate about or something that is necessary for your comfortable survival. Unfulfilled goals are one of the biggest reasons of unhappiness in life. When you try to identify the gap between your desired life and reality, you will be able to find your unachieved goals.

In the previous chapter on subconscious beliefs, we comprehended the stumbling blocks that prevent freethinking. From there, you must have realised that you, too, are an equally deserving candidate. Here is a chance to break your present reality and do something to merge with your dream reality. Make goals that expand your talent and are not merely limited to what you are capable of today. Resolve your doubts, spread your wings, and fly high, this time!

Your goals should be wholesome—covering the various aspects of your life. You cannot just excel in making money and have a deteriorating health or crippling family relationships. This makes life incomplete. Here, I have listed a few areas where the gap between reality and dreams can be bridged and peace of mind and soul can be achieved. Your goals can be beyond this list as well.

- Relationships: family, friends, colleagues, social, etc.
- Career: knowledge, education, creativity, money, skills, job, business, etc.
- Environment: house, needs, comfort, neighbourhood, etc.
- Body: health, fitness, diet, exercise, etc.
- Mind: intellectual awareness, contribution to society, etc.

- Soul: spiritual awareness, inner well-being, etc.
- Better self: confidence, honesty, compassion, gratitude, etc.

Examine these areas to find the missing link. Identify the areas of resentments and improve them by including it in your list of goals. If you have zeal and a burning desire to achieve your goal, it's easier to feed your mind for its accomplishment. An intense emotion like passion can shift your thoughts towards your aspirations and change its intensity. If you are not passionate about your goals, you will not be able to focus on your thoughts. As a result, your thoughts and actions will not synchronise and this will delay the manifestation process. Simply put—if you do not want it bad enough, it will not be in your thoughts prominently and therefore, it will not manifest that easily. And because of this reason, you may start feeling that it doesn't work!

When I quit my job in search of finding a more meaningful purpose of my life, I was not sure of what to do. So, under the influence of my parents, I started preparing for a doctorate programme. Since I was not passionate about pursuing a doctorate programme at that time, even after applying the ABR formula, I could not give it my 100% despite all my efforts. I realised that I was moving in the wrong direction. So, I changed what I had been asking for. I asked the universe to bring to me something that my heart desires; something that will give me inner peace and satisfaction. To my surprise, a few days later, a deep desire to write a book surfaced! It crossed my mind frequently until I realised that this is a wakeup call for me, and gathered the courage to turn it into reality.

But do not rush. Take a week's time to understand the difference between your present state and your expectations from the future. You can meditate and ask your inner voice to show you the right path (given in detail in Chapter 6). If you are lost, it will be difficult for you to find your real aspirations amidst the usual humdrum. Look for a peaceful and inspiring environment to contemplate on your goals. Here are some terms so that you can better grasp the concepts involved when setting out for a goal.

a) Real Goals and Artificial Goals

Make real goals that you own and which come to you naturally. Goals that come from within you are your true desires. They make you passionate enough to manifest them. It is this fire, this zeal that drives you towards the completion of your goals with dedication. Remember, your mind will follow wherever your heart goes.

Goals forced by society or borrowed from it are not yours; they are what I call artificial goals. They are the goals which the media, government, advertisers, society, or peer pressure has decided for you. There is nothing wrong in following them until you are not getting trapped in despair, unjust competition, or inferiority complex. Also, when the desires are not coming from within you, you are not eager, motivated, or disciplined enough to achieve them.

So, before forming your list, question yourself that whether you are being true to yourself or just copying from someone else's goal list? Reflect on this fact and maybe, you will find one of your real goals in this quest.

b) End Goals and Mean Goals

End goals, as the name suggest, are your ultimate desires from life. Mean goals are one of the many paths you take to reach your ultimate goal. Whenever you have a goal in front of you, ask yourself, "Why do I want to fulfil this goal?" You will get some answer. Keep questioning yourself until you find the end goal that which truly lights you up and beyond which you will stop chasing your mean goal. End goals provide you with more clarity and enthusiasm and make you action-oriented. Identifying end goals can open up many paths (mean goals) for its fulfilment.

Mean goals are necessary milestones but not the final destination. When you know the difference between your end goals and mean goals, you will not get lost in the process. You will know when you have achieved a mean goal and how far you need to travel to get to your end goal. The following examples illustrate this:

- Shree is working part-time to do some extra savings is a mean goal. She wants these savings for a family holiday so that she can spend some joyous moments with her kids and have memories for a life-time. This is her end goal.
- Om aims to work out for seven hours weekly and have a well-balanced, wholesome diet; this is his mean goal. His end goal is to continue his passion for winning marathons even in his 60s.

❖ Listing Your Goals

Global leadership expert, Robin Sharma, said in one of his podcasts, "Things that get written get done." Once identified, it is a good practise to list down your goals. Writing makes the goals specific. Specificity helps you observe more vividly. The better the grip on your thoughts, the better the creation process will be.

For this purpose, create your 'Happiness Diary'. Use a new notebook or a diary with pages and binding the way you like. It should appear good to you whenever you hold it. If you are purchasing it, buy two, because one can be used as a gratitude journal later on. In the diary, leave few pages from the beginning and then start listing your goals.

Start with your 3-month, 6-month, and 1-year goals. List all the luxuries you want to enjoy, the adventures you want to pursue, the people you want to meet, the places you want to visit, the emotions and opportunities you want to experience, the skills you want to develop, the fitness level you want to achieve, etc. This can include anything like better health treatment for your parents, finding love or happiness, having a job that supports your family, getting promoted, becoming more confident, expanding business, developing a fantastic hobby, completing your education, excelling in some skill, achieving political greatness, gaining spiritual insight, accomplishing success in sports or arts or science, vacationing on a cruise ship, healing an illness, and so on. Once done with your current 3-month goals, write down your 6-month goals, followed by your 1-year and 3-year goals on new pages. You can even make sections for love, health, job, adventure, self-improvement, etc.

Do not be in a hurry to write down your goals. It may happen that with time, your list might change due to some alterations in your preferences and priorities. Rewrite the list then. But keep in mind that you do not change the list too often. It will be like going to a restaurant and changing your order too frequently and then returning home empty stomach.

While preparing the list, make sure that you are open about asking anything you want. Each goal in your list should be free from the judgement 'How?' Do not hesitate as you won't be penalised for writing down your life's ambitions! With courage and enthusiasm, take this first step.

Asking does not necessarily have to be in the form of some wish list. It is not a rule written on stone. But since we are talking about effective approaches towards asking, it is highly recommended that you make your happiness dairy. It will keep your spirits high. It will give clarity about your goals and confidence in the process. As you achieve one milestone after another, the small ticks that you put in front of each goal will prove to be highly satisfying.

Your goals should be formulated intelligently so that they cover every aspect of your desire. Never repeat your goals like a parrot. They are not mere words, but rather strings of faith and emotions. For this purpose, a few points to take care of while writing down your goals are as follows:

a) Make Affirmative Goals

Affirmation is the act of stating something positively and clearly. While listing down your goals, make them into affirmative (positive) sentences. For example, "I don't want to fall sick" should be replaced with "I am healthy". Thoughts do not interpret words like don't, can't, never, hardly, little, nor, ever, maybe, etc.; they only take the message. As an observer, you cannot observe words and can only observe the message 'falling sick'. And while thinking of sickness, how can you be healthy? Whenever possible, avoid words that carry a negative meaning with them. As soon as you put down a word in ink, your mind creates a picture of it. Therefore, the words should carry an affirmative meaning. This applies at every step, whether you are asking, believing, or receiving. Start your affirmation with 'I' or 'I Am' followed by a positive verb. There can be many other forms of sentences as well, but try to write in the present tense and use positive words.

Example:

- I am doing the best for my daughter's education.
- I take the right financial decisions for my business development.

Affirmation will help in the following ways:

- When used with conviction, affirmations can brush off self-impeding beliefs and thoughts.
- Using them together with the next two steps of the ABR process can create new neural networks in the brain that would correspond to new thought patterns.

If your affirmation seems to be conflicting, there could be two reasons: either your belief is contradictory to your affirmation or you find it morally wrong. Correct the situation else the intensity of the affirmation will be lost.

b) Add Outcomes and Time Frames to Your Goals

While forming affirmation, if you can add the outcome of that goal, it will be an added advantage. Every time you read your affirmation, you will be reminded of what wonderful results await you once you achieve your goal. This will keep you highly motivated and involved in the process of asking.

Adding time frame to sentences helps in timely decision making. It creates a positive pressure, necessary to keep you moving.

Example:

- Each week, I am committed to closing sufficient sales deals with my clients, which helps grow my business profile by 40% in the following three months.

But a key point to consider while adding time frames to your goals is that they are only recommended when you are sure or confident about the timeline of your goals to some extent. Otherwise, time constraints become a cause of unnecessary fretting about the completion of your goal. It restricts the free flow of energy by keeping you chained to your goal. Also, spiritually speaking, the energy of the universe may have a better time plan for you than the one you decided. So, add time frames that are not too restrictive to cause discouragement or desperation.

c) Specificity of Your Goals

Some practitioners of thought-power encourage you to write goals having exact make, model, label name, and quantity. In my opinion, being very specific about the quality or quantity of your goals may demoralise you. It may create feelings of scarcity and doubt.

Therefore, it is extremely important as to how you form your affirmations and what you include in your visualisations. Very specific details may cause more reality inertia and uncertainty in subconscious beliefs. This will result in a harder manifestation process. Instead of narrowing down your choices, form goals that have a greater probability of fulfilment. Hence, it is better that while writing goals, be specific about its quality or quantity, in a big-picture sense.

Consider the following examples:

- I want to switch my job.
- I have a new job at XYZ Inc. as a senior manager of the sales department with an annual salary of INR 25,00,000.
- I have a new job at a *reputed firm* as a senior manager of the sales department with *very rewarding earnings*.

The first sentence is very vague, while the second one is too specific and traps you into too many details. On the other hand, the third option helps you with making believable goals. It is clear to the extent of giving a necessary positive push to you. Your goal is open to any firm, from a pool of 'reputed firms' and it also does not limit you to 'INR 25,00,000'. This decreases the reality inertia and also satisfies your beliefs. Thus, making the process of believing and receiving (ABR process) remains easy and accessible for you.

Sometimes, the higher power has planned a different path for you. When this happens, your specific goals may not get fulfilled and will cause unnecessary frustration in life. You have to have faith that the energy of the universe will send your way that which is best for you and your soul's purpose. Instead of forcing your goals, align yourself with the process of creation by making supportive affirmations (Asking), visualisations (Believing), and performing actions (Receiving).

Mention only those details of your goals which are extremely important for you and for other details use positive words, emotions, and adjectives. Leave the rest on the energy of the universe to decide on your behalf.

In some cases, you may be concerned about the label, time frame, and model of your goal. In such cases, go ahead by adding specificities to your goal, if they really matter a lot and are necessary.

Example:

- I will perform excellent in my match with the XYZ team next Monday.
- I will get admission in one of the best universities in the country which will enhance my knowledge and career growth to the fullest.

❖ The Power of 'I Am'

'I Am' are the two most powerful words that you can utter to change your life. The beauty of this phrase is that its use is completely under your control, like your thoughts. You are the master of your 'I Am'. Only you can use it for yourself and say what you feel about yourself. Whatever you attach to your 'I Am' is what you believe about yourself. So be careful as your 'I Am' can bring you victory as well as defeat. Affirm to yourself with feelings such as "I am a wonderful person", and you will feel great. Affirm to yourself something like "I am a loser", and you will feel like one. This power is at work throughout your life.

'I Am' helps you believing in something and then receiving it. It gives you the strength and confidence to identify your potential and set your goals. In the words of Joel Osteen (Pastor), "Whatever follows the 'I Am' will eventually find you."

Western culture believes 'I Am' is the name of God. This energy is dwelling within each of us and it has empowered us to conquer our difficulties and reach the pinnacle. The word *Soham*, which comes from Hindu Sanskrit texts and means 'I Am He', also carries the same meaning. I do not consider myself qualified to talk further about the origin of this word, but from the little I understand based on my research, I can conclude that when you say the word Soham (I Am He), you remove all dualities and identify yourself with the universe. When you say 'I Am' and affix it with something, the bond between you and that thing becomes strong enough to draw it towards you.

'I Am' is your consciousness believing in what it is and what it can do. When you use 'I', it is like a command given to the mind. For example, "I am worthy" tells the mind what it is and how it has to be. Every time you say it to yourself, you strengthen your beliefs and move towards proactive thinking.

You can use this word power to Ask, Believe, and Receive (ABR process) from the energy of the universe. If possible, your goals should start with 'I am'. For example,

"I am happy" is a better way to ask for happiness than "I want to be happy". In his book, *The Power of I AM*, David Allen suggests to repeat these words quietly and with feelings until you lose consciousness of the world around you and get thrilled with the understanding that you actually are what you desire for.

I have used powerful 'I Am' affirmations to find my purpose in life. Every night before going to sleep and many times during the day, I would say to myself the affirmations that I formulated for this purpose. I don't know why the mind resonates so much with the phrase 'I Am'. But from my personal experience, I have realised that it gives you confidence in self and the mind gets absorbed in the process of deliberate creation. 'I Am' gears up your internal world for outer success.

Never use 'I Am' to say something negative about you. If something goes wrong, people are in the habit of whimpering things like "Oh, I am stupid", "I am so fat", "I am not capable", "I am not beautiful", etc. Do not add anything to your 'I Am', which you do not want to experience in your life. Do not add flaws and complains to your 'I Am'. Why say the opposite of what you want?

One of my friends always used to tell me things like "I am not beautiful anymore", "I am becoming fat", "I have wrinkled skin", and so on. It took me some time to make her realise that when she is not beautiful in her own eyes, then how can she expect her husband to find her pretty? You need to love yourself first and only then the world will love you. You need to adore yourself and respect yourself. What you believe about yourself will reflect in your words and thoughts and whatever is in your thoughts will be in your life.

❖ Autosuggestion

It is an extremely reliable way of communicating your desires to every ounce of your body. Once you feed your mind with what you want, each cell in your body will be notified about what is expected from it. We saw in Chapter 3 that self-talk or autosuggestion happens all the time and it builds up your beliefs. Such autosuggestions are a great way of communicating with your mind about your affirmations. You can use this process to sow the seeds for desired thoughts in your mind. The mind and the energy of the universe then conspire to bring you closer to the finish line.

Autosuggestions are powerful tools for developing habits. I have been using them to develop advantageous habits that can bring me closer to something on my wish list. Autosuggestions have helped me strengthen my willpower, made me follow my writing schedule, and many such things.

It is important that when you use autosuggestions, you emotionalise them. Say it with feelings in your mind and say it with joy. The goals should not be read like a parrot mugging up what his master teaches him. Emotionalise what you are reading. Read your goals with a feeling that you deserve them. Also, while reading, trust yourself and feel happy about your ambitions. With half-hearted efforts, you can't expect overwhelming results. Think about your goal list while jogging, driving, travelling by train, waiting at the coffee shop, etc. Impregnate each cell of your body with your aim . . . after all, it is their aim as well! Louise L. Hay, author of the bestselling book, *You Can Heal Your Life*, suggests doing the affirmations while standing in front of a mirror. Looking into your eyes and affirming to yourself is a real motivator. When you say it directly to your face, you start accepting it.

Many times, the mind gets busy with some negative self-talk about scarcity, sickness, hatred, jealousy, etc. Such a self-talk is an intruder into your mind as it makes you mentally weak from within. From now on, whenever you find the time, do some money-talk, abundance-talk, health-talk, happy-talk, etc. Believe me, it will elevate your spirits and make you feel like you are riding on a merry-go-round.

Research suggests that positive repetitive thoughts help in recovery from upsetting and traumatic events and depression. Also, these promote healthy behaviours and prepare you by planning ahead. (Edward R. Watkins, 2008)

The repetition of your goal list can be done as per your schedule. Studies show that getting thoughts embedded into your subconscious mind is easy when the mind is in alpha state. It is the state just before falling asleep and just after waking up. The alpha state of mind is said to be the state of visualisation, finding solutions, and getting inner guidance. The mind is receptive to suggestions in this state. Autosuggestion in this state is like self-hypnosis, where you can direct your brain and feed it with desired thoughts.

When on your bed, instead of thinking about what went wrong during the day, think about what best you can do the next day to fulfil your goals. If you sleep with a positive mindset, you wake up with one. It then becomes easier for you to carry that mindset throughout the day.

Do not waste this time scrolling through your phone. What you want in life is not more post on social media rather the fulfilment of your goals. This is the time when the mind is vulnerable to taking up any data that you provide it. American psychologist Archibald D. Hart writes in his book, *The Digital Invasion: How Technology is Shaping You and Your Relationships*, "Most Christians have been taught that prayer and devotional time should be the first activity of their day. In reality, for most of us, it is to check our email. For others, it is voice mail, text messages, tweets, and the latest notifications." The Internet and media leave you craving for more stuff, more consumerism, and more pessimist news. It does not satisfy your goals or provides you with inner peace. Rather you sink into a feeling of lack, sorrow, and competition. Your precious moments of being in your alpha state of mind should be reserved for your wishes, dreams, goals, life, and happiness and not the opposite.

Let's move on to the next step of the ABR formula which is about consciously designing all the aspects of your goals so that the platter served to you has what you expect from life.

Chapter 6

'Believe' in Yourself

"Imagination at work."
—General Electric tagline

Once you have decided what to extract from the pool of waves present around you, it's time for observation. Asking is about making a choice and believing is about providing details about that choice so that the manifestation process can be set into motion. At this step of creation, you actually try to observe your reality through imagination.

Believing is an extremely important part of the three-step success formula. Whatever you have asked, you have to be sure of achieving it. This is the step where your proactive thinking becomes of vital importance. When you believe in your goals, you are thrilled, passionate, excited, and joyous. This combination of happy emotions easily makes you a proactive creator.

By believing, you confirm that your choice can be converted into reality. It assures that you have faith, you are confident, and you have no doubts regarding the creation process. Believing gives the spirit to move mountains and reach for the sky!

As soon as you list your goals, you have to start the process of believing. You have to believe that whatever you have ordered from the universe's storehouse is already yours. When you proactively decide the aspects of your reality, your subconscious mind starts giving you the signs and information needed for the completion of your goals.

Approach towards Effective Believing

At the core of the process of believing lies the act of visualisation. Believing in your goals comes before receiving so that the picture you have in your mind fills you with enough passion to act immediately. Listed below are few approaches for better observation of your reality and for a better creation process.

- ❖ **Visualisation of Your Goals**

  The imaginative faculty of the mind is responsible for every invention done by humanity. From conquering the sky and the ocean to finding solutions to hunger and disease, humans have achieved immense growth in diverse areas of science and technology by deploying their imagination skills. If you are serious about making a change, it is not enough to have some general desire for improving your life. For this, you have to strike a balance between mental and physical actions to achieve your targets.

  In this step of believing, you will be forming images of the things, people, and experiences that are listed in your goal list. Visualisation will help you live your future in the present! It is like having the remote control of your life in your hands. Visualisation is the actual creative process behind the three steps—Ask, Believe, and Receive. To understand this, think about an architect with a contract for building a luxury resort. Now, until the guy has some mental picture of what this resort would look like, he won't be able to initiate the project.

  Thus, an image gives clarity and direction to proceed in. You have to create pictures of your desires in your mind. The car you want to have, the house you want to purchase, the qualities you want in your life partner, and so on. The clearer your desires are in the world within, the better they will appear in the world outside. Emotions and details should fuel your mental images. You should be passionate enough to sustain that picture in your mind as often as possible. Detailed imagination and focused repetitions will help you in the process. As the picture in your mind will unfold, so will the path that leads towards it.

The way you rethink your past via your memories, you can think of your future via imagining it. The pleasantness involved with the latter is that you still have time to mould it as per your preferences.

Few points to consider for better visualisation of your goals are:

a) Overcoming Doubts

Remember how easy it was for you as a kid to pretend to be a doctor by holding a toy stethoscope around your neck or becoming an astronaut by getting in a colourful box with your head in the air. I remember pretending to be a celebrity who is being interviewed by a journalist! At that time, things seemed easy and you were not scared of visualising yourself in a position you wanted to be in. Let yourself be that little kid once again, who is not afraid of imagining big goals! Being fearless in your visualisation is important. If your visualisation and beliefs don't match, it won't turn out to be a perfect manifestation.

To explain this further, I would like to share one of my own manifestation experiences. In the last semester of my post-graduation, I listed four job-related goals. I was able to fulfil three of my goals (getting placement in a reputed MNC, getting my joining letter before the completion of the semester, and getting a job in a city of my choice) by successfully applying the tips I have shared in this book. The fourth goal was getting a salary package of INR 30,00,000 per annum. Being a product of one of the premium educational institutes of the country, getting this package was not impossible. But it was way too much for my subconscious mind to believe in. Despite all the ABR steps that I tried to follow, my inner chatterbox kept telling me, "Hold on! This is unattainable!" In the end, I was unable to manifest my specific and desired salary package. I realised that something went wrong while applying the thought-power. I went back to the basics of this concept. After studying various resources on the subject, I realised my flaw. I wasn't following the very cardinal essence of the whole process. I was focusing on my desired salary half-heartedly. Deep in my heart, I lacked faith in the energy of the universe and myself. I finally understood the importance of beliefs but the hard way!

Some of you who are already aware of the process of asking, believing, and receiving may have had a similar experience. This might have led you to the conclusion: "Manifestation never happened, even after focused thinking!" Do not blame it on the power of your thoughts. Thought-power is never wrong. It is you who is unable to apply it correctly. Remember, your fears and impossible goals are just some false beliefs.

Whenever in doubt during visualisation, ask yourself, "How will I feel after accomplishing this goal?" The answer will infuse a flow of positive thoughts and feelings. This will strengthen your will to visualise. In the last chapter, I gave you an example of having the goal of possessing the latest black Mercedes. Initially, imagining this goal may be challenging for some. If so, ask yourself, "How will it feel to take your wife on a dinner date in your own Mercedes?" or "How will it feel dropping your kid to school in your brand-new dream car?" Answers to such questions increase your creativity and help you connect to the imaginary scenario efficiently.

The examples I keep quoting are not the only goals that can be manifested. The fact is that each person's goals are different. Simply put—your life, your goals, your imagination. But if your present hardships do not allow you to envision big goals, then start with something small. Start with observing and creating a basic necessity for you. Start with realising any one of your daily goals. If you are in a state where you are unable to afford 3 meals per day, then your goal can be of having a fulfilling dinner. It completely depends upon your needs, as to what you would like to create in your life through a positive thought-cycle. It is not necessary that you only have to visualise a big house or a million-dollar income.

b) Using Pictures and Drawings

It is said, "A picture is as good as a thousand words." So why not use it to your benefit? The brain processes visual information faster and it is easier to recall. Visual memory creates a greater impact and has longevity. Therefore, looking at the pictures of your goals will create a profound impact on your brain.

You can cut out pictures from magazines, catalogues, newspapers, or goggle them. You can stick these pictures on your vision board or in your happiness diary. If you do not find a desired picture of your goal, then draw one for yourself. You don't need to be some artist; a simple picture representing what you want, pasted on your vision board, can work wonders in your life. You can also collect the pictures in some box and take a look every day. I personally prefer sticking them in my happiness diary as it keeps them private and it is easier to carry them while travelling. You can also divide these pictures and put some in your happiness diary and some on your vision board. Do whatever suits you. Your vision board should be at a place that is easily accessible every day, so that each time you see your vision board, it will remind your mind, body, and soul of the synchronous roles they have to play in order to attain your goals.

Once you have the picture in your happiness diary or vision board, you may write some details about it. For instance, the timeline, action plan, its qualities, the outcomes, your feelings, etc. Try describing the quality or quantity together with your feelings—the job you want, your ideal lifestyle, the number of goals you want to score on the football ground, etc.

c) Creative Visualisation: From Reel Life to Real Life

Creative visualisation, as the name suggests, is a visualisation method where you creatively use all your five senses to pull out the details of a scenario you want to visualise. Scientifically, these visualisation practices are known as 'Visual Motor Rehearsal'. Authors Esther and Jerry Hicks suggest that even a focused imagination, for as little as 17 seconds, can set the creation forces into motion!

Whether you have the winning trophy in your hand or you are simply imagining about it in your mind, both the events fire up the same neural pathways in the brain. Visualisation is a powerful tool used by athletes, dancers, sportsmen, etc. for the mental rehearsal of what is coming in the future. Mental rehearsal helps you pre-imagine the future scenario, where you can get insights on how to deal with the actual situation. Through this way, the cognitive processes in the brain are activated and the brain performs a rehearsal before entering the real-life stage. Creative visualisation also helps in better use of the right hemisphere of the brain, which otherwise is harnessed less than the left hemisphere by most people.

Famous sportsmen and celebrities have used this technique to prepare themselves better for their challenges and achieve success. Muhammad Ali, Arnold Schwarzenegger, Tiger Woods, Oprah Winfrey, Jim Carrey, Will Smith, Jay Z, Lady Gaga, and many other big names advocate the power of visualisation in enhancing their capabilities. You, too, can make use of this mental game to live a better life.

Visualising Process

Once you close your eyes, pick up one goal that you would like to visualise. It can be something from your goal list, a solution to some problem, or some experience you want to have. Now, you have to imagine in your mind a large TV screen, a few feet in front of you, playing a movie called *My Life*. Here you are both the director and the hero of the movie. Visualise whatever scenes you would like to have in your movie and say 'cut' to any unwanted thoughts. Start with your affirmation and then move on step-by-step to all the happenings related to your goal. Imagine all the compelling details of the process, actions, and achievement of your goal. The more details you give during the process, the better the match it will be with your desired reality.

In the words of motivational speaker and author, Lisa Nichols, "Your visualisations should be 'Emotionally-fuelled visualisations.'" Make visualisations a full-body experience. Your imagination has wings and colours. So, paint your goals grandly. Breathe life into your dreams. Also, try involving all your senses. See colours. You can imagine your action-plan, what others are saying to you, how excited you are, what conversations you are having, how people are congratulating you, how your loved ones are benefiting from your achievement, the feeling of gratitude this accomplishment will bring, etc. Notice the smell in the air, the colour of your dress, the background, the surroundings, etc. You have to feel, touch, taste, hear, and see the images of your goal. You have to live it in your mind! And when it actually happens, it will be a déjà vu for you! Soak yourself in those images each day till they no longer remain a virtual reality. Increase the details but do not change it entirely, else your focus will be scattered.

If you find it difficult to visualise the end results, you can start by visualising yourself performing the actions that will lead to the desired results. This will also help you get into the habit of taking actions that are necessary for the completion of your goals. Just remember, the limitations of your achievement lie in the limitations of your imagination.

Not everyone is vision-dominant during their visualisations. For some, other senses like smell, taste, and sound are more dominant. Use more of any of your dominant sense. The results will remain equally good.

These visualisations can be practised as per your schedule. But like affirmations, the best time to practise include:

- Just before going to bed and just after getting up in the morning.
- During meditation sessions.
- Allocating 5-10 minutes of visualisation time in silence when you have spare time.

Whenever an upsetting event comes your way and disturbs you, say 'STOP' and bring into picture the mental imagery you have mapped out for one of your goals. At first, you will have blurred mental images, but with time, as your practise continues, the details of your mental pictures will become clearer. Like a muscle, you can strengthen your visualisation power. The way your emotions empower your thoughts, visualisations empower your affirmations. Creative visualisations gear you up to perform actions.

Let's see a few examples:

- John sprained his right foot while climbing the stairs. Together with medication, John decides to use creative visualisation to heal his foot sooner. He visualises himself playing his favourite sport—football. He imagines scoring a goal by hitting the ball with his right foot and hears cheers from his team. He also visualises coming home and taking his daughter to the park where he is running behind her while she is chasing a butterfly with open arms. He then catches hold of his daughter and swings her in the air playfully.

- Mahi is suffering from severe headache. She uses the visualisation technique to return to her healthy bodily state. She uses symbolism to treat her pain. She takes a golden coloured balm or light from the pool of energy fields surrounding her and as she rubs this balm on her head, she feels the pain going away. She repeats this technique a few times and waits for her headache to go away.

  Such symbolic actions can be used to cure any disease, together with medication. This provides quicker healing. Once you develop faith by targeting smaller problems, you can move on to cure chronic illnesses as well. These visualisation healings are not a replacement of doctor's prescription, but rather they are there to assist the healing process.

- If you are searching for true love, list down the traits that you want to have in your life partner. You can visualise having coffee with that person or a situation where you are telling him/her about your favourite holiday destination. Imagine your partner coming to pick you up after work or how you both are enjoying preparing a brunch together or going out for movies etc.

- Suppose your wish list includes buying a new office space. You can recce your preferred locality. You can visualise the floor on which your office will be situated, the size of the lobby, the number of cubicles you want on each floor, the interior of your own cabin, the painting behind your office desk, the furniture you would love to have, the indoor plants in the office lobby, the café corner, etc. Imagine hearing the phone ringing on your work desk, smelling the fresh coffee beans at the office café, feeling the warmth of your new cabin, etc.

- If you have a problem to solve, turn your problem into a project. Your goal is to imagine finding a solution to this problem. Analyse and pull out all that you have in your mind as an answer. Imagine whatever you can and then leave the rest for your higher intelligence to solve. Finish your visualisation by requesting the energy of the universe and your mind to show you the right path. Then once you get up, walk as if the problem is a past, and the solution is your new reality.
- You can visualise yourself getting rid of some unwanted emotions like anger, sadness, etc. Imagine yourself becoming calmer and more compassionate. You can take it to the next step by imagining yourself as a person who is loved, admired, and has an influential personality.

Once you have finished your visualisation sessions, move out and embrace your new reality. Do not overthink. Start behaving as if your request has already been fulfilled. Acting as if you have it establishes harmony between your observation and the creation process. Do all those things mentally that you would do after achieving your goals. You should hold it in your mind in order to hold it in your hands. Live in that house mentally, give that presentation mentally, launch your business mentally, and play with your healthy child mentally. Own your goals in your mental picture so firmly that you bend the reality in your favour. Create that happiness, health, and wisdom—all in your mind.

Creative visualisation is a practice which is highly innovative. There is an infinite possibility of variations. It is impossible for me to give you everything here. You have to find for yourself how well you can decorate your imagination for finding happiness, action plans, solutions, etc.

d) Visualise Your 'Big Day'

Many a time, you come across situations where you have to display your talent or knowledge. It can be writing an exam, convincing your manager/head, public speaking, presentations, interviews, group discussions, meeting strangers, persuading clients, giving auditions, sports performance, competing for an award, etc. These are the times when, out of fear and low self-esteem, you may experience disappointment.

Whenever you are preparing yourself for any such big day, together with the necessary actions, practise creative visualisation. Visualise the outcome of your success. You can visualise your great performance, the benefits you will get, cheering from the audience, the impact of that event, the person you will become after that, and so on. You can also list these benefits in your happiness diary. Imagining the successful completion of the event will boost your confidence and make you stronger and passionate.

Some Research:

- Astonishing research by V. K. Ranganathan et al., 2004 and Wan X. Yao et al., 2013, concluded that kinaesthetic imagery (imagining actions and movements) helped increase muscle strength of the targeted muscles of the patients by 35% and 10.8% respectively.
- A research on chronic stroke patients having long-term motor impairment was conducted by H. C. Dijkerman et al., 2004. A group of patients was asked to visualise moving tokens from their impaired arm. After 4 weeks of this visual rehearsal, the group showed 14% improvement in their motor task.
- Dr O. Carl Simonton (1942-2009), pioneered in the mind-body healing process for treating cancer. His research demonstrated that medication when used with desired mental visualisations, relaxation exercises, and meditation, increased the life expectancy of cancer patients. Later, he went on to establish the Simonton Cancer Centre to provide physiological and emotional support to cancer patients.
- Dr Denis Waitley has trained champions from many fields for the Visual Motor Imagery rehearsal before their actual event. He has several stories to share from Olympic champions, to sales achievers, youth groups, and NASA astronauts. His work confirmed that the mind is unable to distinguish between imagination and reality.

❖ Meditation

Just imagine yourself sitting at your workstation in a fish market and trying to concentrate on your project. Now imagine the same workstation and working on the same project, but in your office. Which environment would you prefer to complete that task or make a business decision? To have focused thoughts, to affirm, and to visualise, the mind needs a peaceful environment. A mind consumed with the rush of daily chores and despair from the world around is unable to focus. Only a focused mind can produce focused thoughts. Meditation is like a healthy diet of peace for your mind.

In today's scenario, every day you have to deal with various issues at a time, from your toddler's vaccination appointment to a client meeting in a different city and therefore, giving some rest to your busy mind is necessary. Meditation will enhance your clarity and performance. If you want to change your life, you have to start with your thoughts, and to start with the thoughts, you need to have a focused mind. Meditation is one of the most potent tool that can help you concentrate your thoughts for unidirectional thinking.

Meditation is an ancient practice that has been used by learned of East and West for thousands of years. It takes your mind into a peaceful state, free of any gloomy or obstructive thoughts. Meditation helps you sort out unwanted thoughts so that the brain is more receptive to positive and clear thinking. It is like cleaning the junk files from your database. It infuses feelings of joy, excitement, satisfaction, and gratitude into your life. It revitalises you. It is like a mini-vacation for your mind that you can celebrate each day! Meditation is like a miracle drug that eliminates toxic thoughts from your system without leaving any side effects.

As you clean your body by bathing each day, you should also clean your mind by meditating each day. Through meditation, you can become restful but alert and feed your subconscious mind with the preferred thoughts during this state.

The brain is an electrochemical organ, displaying its electrical activity in the form of brainwaves. A calmer brain emits alpha and theta waves. These are the states of higher subconscious creativity, intuition, blissfulness, concentration, awareness, and imagination. And through meditation, we are able to achieve these states. Research has also shown that meditation has ample health benefits like better psychological and cardiovascular health.

If you try to sit quietly for 10 minutes to visualise one of your goals, your mind will jump from one thought to another. Your attention will be diverted to various directions. The monkey-mind is common to every individual except those who have learnt to control it. Practise can strengthen the meditative state of your mind. When you are able to concentrate on one single thought for a desired amount of time, you become a powerful observer for the creation of your reality. Just like the sunlight passing through a lens at a specific angle can burn a paper, your unidirectional focus can spark fruitful changes in your life.

If you are inclined to have some deep knowledge of meditation then a few recommendations are *A Million Thoughts* by Om Swami and *The Science of Enlightenment* by Shinzen Young.

Shinzen Young, a world-renowned meditation teacher, talks about a bitter part of meditation in his book, *The Science of Enlightenment*: "I live with the knowledge that most people will never have what they so easily could achieve. I know that the demands of daily life will convince them they cannot set aside even a few moments to develop that one skill [Meditation] that will make it possible for them to optimally respond to those demands." So, if there is anyone out there who thinks that meditation is not their cup of tea, give it a try for the sake of the abundant life you wish for.

a) Medisation: Visualisation during Meditation

One of the best practices that you can take away from this book is what I call 'Medisation'. Visualisations can be done at any time as per one's suitability, but from my experience, I have concluded that the best time for visualisation is during meditation and thus the term Medisation. Meditation makes the mind serene and affirmations and visualisations done with a calm mind leave a greater impact and thus connecting to your goals becomes a smooth process then. According to Dr Joe Dispenza, "Meditating is a means for you to move beyond your analytical mind so that you can access your subconscious mind. That's crucial, since the subconscious is where all your bad habits and behaviours that you want to change reside."

Different meditation experts have suggested different ways of doing it. For some, meditation is a way of achieving the state of mind which is free of thoughts, while for some, it is the state where you have free flow of thoughts, and for still others, it is a state where you concentrate on one single thought, and so on. Some meditations work by focusing on your breath, others on some mantra or deity or image or word.

These all are a passive form of meditation that aim to quiet the mind and then stay with that bliss. But what we will practise here is an 'active' form of meditation; a meditation where after calming down the mind, you will make use of this profound state for creating your reality. Active meditation is for today's time. A time where your 24 hours are divided into tasks, goals, meetings, cooking meals, changing diapers, raising stubborn adolescents, and then at the end of the day, craving for some peace of mind and me-time.

D. Goleman and R. J. Davidson in their book, *The Science of Meditation*, have described meditation into two broad groups—wide and deep path. The wide meditation is the modern take on meditation where we harness the superficial but immense benefits of meditation. The deep path is the intense mediation practices performed by yogis and monks. What we are talking about is the wide path of meditation.

b) Steady Breath Medisation

The first stage of the medisation process is a meditation to calm your mind. There are many ways to achieve this meditative state, like discussed above. This stage can be completed by performing any kind of meditation that works best for you. You can find several types of meditation procedures on YouTube and other mobile apps. There are meditation courses led by good practitioners and gurus. You can also try any of these apart from the one shared here and settle down for the most comfortable one. Through trial and error, I have developed a 'steady breath medisation' process for myself, which I found to be very effective. Let's see how it is done.

Steps Involved in Steady Breath Medisation

Step 1

(To know about the science behind this step, please read the notes section at the end. Becoming aware of the rationale behind your actions often increases your willpower for doing them. The analytical mind gets its query resolved and it pulls back and lets faith in. This boosts your meditation practice and you start following it meticulously.)

It is recommended to choose meditation as one of your morning rituals as the mind is comparatively free of dismissive thoughts in the morning. But if you are unable to find time in the morning, practise it any time, whenever you are free. Always practise meditation in a silent environment and in a comfortable position. Start with small sessions and make it a daily habit. Even if you are busy, just spare 15-20 minutes each day for the whole process of medisation. Once you start mastering the skill, this time frame can be further extended.

You are free to adopt any posture that suits you and helps you focus on the process. A common posture is the lotus position. If this is not possible, you can start by simply sitting on a chair with your back straight or on a mat with legs crossed, back straight, and palms on your lap. What is important is to start it and later, you can improve it.

Further, some of you might get drowsy, once the calmness of the process starts overtaking you. In such situations, choose a position that makes you mildly uncomfortable so that you do not drowse off so easily. These tips would significantly help you with your meditation.

Meditating Process

1. Sit in a comfortable position, cross-legged with a straight back, preferably. Loosen your body and try to relax completely.
2. From top to bottom, start paying attention to your body parts and the space around them while feeling them getting relaxed. Pay attention to the centre of your head, forehead, eyes, face, throat, shoulders, hands, chest centre, upper abdomen, lower abdomen, thighs, knees, calves, feet, and toes. As your attention moves from one body part to the other and the space around them, your body keeps sinking into deeper relaxation.
3. Have a smile on your face. Feel good that you have this opportunity to transform yourself. Realise that we all are energy beings, made from the same energy. Realise the depth of this interconnectedness.
4. Start with rhythmic breathing. You have to choose a certain rhythm of inhalation and exhalation that works best for you. The ratio of air taken in to out should be constant throughout. For example, start with a rhythm of four counts of deep inhalation, six counts of deep exhalation, and two counts of halt. This will complete your one cycle of breath. Do the counting in mind. The pace of the counting should be normal, i.e. neither too fast nor too slow. Take care that the periodicity of each inhalation and exhalation cycle should be same throughout the process, i.e. it can be 5-5-2 or 4-6-2 or 6-8-2, etc., but not one cycle of 4-3-2, then the next cycle of 5-7-2 and then 4-8-2. Choose the pace and ratio of the breath that suits you. A preferred one is 5-5-2 but you can also start

with 4-6-2. Maintain the smoothness of the breaths, i.e. inhalation and exhalation should be gentle and slow. Feel the air moving in and out of your body and energising each and every cell of your body.

5. During the whole process, try to focus your attention on your chest centre for maximum benefit. You will notice your chest muscles moving in and out with each cycle of breath. Initially, your mind will wander away, but gently pull it back to your chest centre. At the centre, feel your heart becoming healthy and emotionally sound with each intake of air. Feel love and gratitude for your body and your life and bless your heart. By surging in this positivity, you are deliberately shifting how you feel and how you feel will decide what you will think.

For a 20-minute medisation session, devote the first 10 minutes to rhythmic breathing and the next 10 minutes to step 2. The rhythmic breathing will calm down your internal mind-chatter. Initially, you will take time to de-stress your mind, as it has been in a disorderly state for too long. Be patient. The way exercise tones your muscles, meditation will tone your mind. With daily practise, you will realise that vague thoughts are visiting your mind less frequently. You will develop a better focus on your breathing and chest centre.

Step 2

In the second half of your medisation practice, continue with rhythmic and smooth breathing (you can stop counting now) while following the steps given below:

1. **Gratitude:**

   The incredible process of gratitude is explained in detail in the next chapter. As of now, start with thanking all those things and people that you are grateful to—your family, house, education, wealth, job, business, health, success, friends, food, comfort, etc. Appreciate the presence of these things and people in your life.

2. **Affirmations and Visualisations:**

   We have already talked in detail about how to make affirmations and visualise your future in the previous sections. Your peaceful mind will help in better affirmations and creative visualisations.

   After expressing gratitude, silently repeat your affirmations with emotions a few times. Start with goals as per your present needs or choice or your 3-month goals from your happiness diary. Ask the energy of the universe to bless you with a life of infinite abundance. You can even ask for a better meditation practise or being more disciplined while following your ABR practise.

   Now move on to visualisation. Visualise in your mind a goal that you want to fulfil in the near future. Use all your senses to imagine how marvellous it would be to achieve those pinnacles that you dream about. Once done, have faith and pay gratitude to the energy of the universe for considering your wishes and helping you in their realisation.

3. **Plan Your Day:**

   The last step is to make the plans for today—the most

important day of your life. Yes, start today, right now, and at this point. Chalk out what you can do today to take you an inch closer to your goal. For example, your goal may require you to take an action such as talking to a colleague, making a presentation, surfing the Internet, donating money, feeling gratitude, learning a new skill, developing a hobby, exercising, eating well, making lunch for the family, forgiving someone, going for an outing with friends, etc. It can be simply anything good that can bring you closer to your intentions.

By following these steps, you can maximise your medisation process. But there is a lot more you can extract and attain from this process. This time, which you spend in silence, just with yourself, can be put to use for other advantageous purposes as well such as:

- You can find an answer to an unsolved problem at work. Turn your problem into a project, whose solution you can meditate upon.
- You can make decisions on some particular issues related to family, career, education, etc.
- You can make an action plan for your week or month.

Focus your thoughts on these three steps. Let other random thoughts pass away. With practise, the mind will encounter less uninvited thoughts and you will master the technique. As you get better, you will notice the advantages of medisation throughout the day. You will feel calm, composed, livelier, less irritated, and less distracted. If needed, once the meditation gets over, quickly make a note of any important intuitive guidance or action plan that emerged in your mind.

An important aspect of medisation is to carry that poise and trust throughout the day. Meditating for an hour and then going back to your normal disposition is not done. Keep yourself on check throughout the day, for any unworthy thoughts or emotions trying to hit you. Meditation can make you good at life if you become more responsible for your thinking habits.

This whole process can take anything from 15 minutes to an hour depending on the extent you want to go. Make sure to take time out from your daily chores for this enthralling and life-changing process. It will make you more content with your life and more confident about your plans. Medisation does not take your time away from a busy day but rather increases your potential so that you can do more with the same 24 hours.

Note:

The steady breath meditation is based on heart coherence and controlled breathing pattern. In his book, *Coherence: The Secret Science of Brilliant Leadership,* neuroscientist and leadership expert Dr Alan Watkins explains that the performance of the brain (i.e. feelings, thoughts, emotions, and behaviour) is linked to the physiological performance of the body. If you can control the physiology (normal functions of living organisms and their body parts), you will be able to control what you feel and what you think.

The physiology can be controlled by different body signals. One such method is breathing, which is under your control. The most important aspect of breathing is its rhythm, followed by the smoothness of breath and the location of your attention while breathing. By controlling your breathing pattern, you can affect the heart in a positive manner which then affects your physiology. In fact, controlled breathing has been practised by ancient sages as well. Breathing rhythmically and smoothly increases the 'heart coherence'. A coherent heart is the one where the variation in the time interval between consecutive heartbeats (heart rate variability [HRV]) is smooth. The steady breath medisation technique utilises heart coherence to reach a meditative state of the brain. A few important reasons behind this are:

When the heart is experiencing physiological calmness, it syncs the brain into coherence too. As a result, the brain moves from beta state to alpha state. This is a state of calmness, creativity, and intuition. From here, with practise, one might move to theta to delta state, the higher states of consciousness responsible for psychic insights and mystical experiences. A brain with coherent brain waves aids your directional thinking, affirmations, visualisations, problem-solving skills, and peace of mind.

The heart can independently process emotions and lead your brain to match those emotions. By focusing on your chest centre with positivity and love, you make your heart more coherent and shift yourself upwards on the emotional scale. Thus, by intentionally creating a positive-emotion loop, you assist in the process of creation by being in the right energy zone.

Chaotic, incoherent heart signals, caused by internal or external factors, degrade your cognitive, social, and physical performance. It can drain you emotionally, hamper your thinking ability and affect your behaviour and performance. Since the purpose of meditation is to provide a wholesome wellness effect, practising a heart coherence meditation takes care of your heart, brain, and body.

Heart coherence affects the body mentally, physically, and emotionally and promotes healing.

Some Research:

- A research conducted by Dr Eric Schadt and team, published in *Nature's Translational Psychiatry*, concluded that meditation has long-term benefits on health and emotions than vacationing, which has short-term benefits on well-being.
- A 2014 review study performed by Newberg et al., enumerates the benefits of meditation for treating neurodegenerative diseases (progressive degeneration of nerve cells) by improving cognition and memory in patients.
- A study conducted on mindfulness meditation by Britta K. Holzel et al., 2011, suggested the increase in the concentration of grey matter in brain regions responsible for learning, memory, emotional regulation, and perspective taking.
- A larger portion of research faculty has undergone research to demonstrate the effectiveness of meditation practices in reducing symptoms of depression (Teasdale et al., 2000), chronic pain (Grossman et al., 2007), substance abuse (Bowen et al., 2006), and improved quality of life (Carmody and Baer, 2008).
- Studies on meditation reflect that meditation is also associated with reducing the brain's self-

related thinking and mind-wandering (Bishop et al., 2004, Brewer, Worhunsky, et al., 2011, Kathleen A. Garrison, et al., 2015). Reduced mind-wandering leads to a happier life and increased concentration.

Chapter 7

'Receive' by Performing Actions

"The infinite wonders of the universe are revealed to us in exact measure as we are capable of receiving them."
—Helen Keller (activist)

As you move forward on the track of realising your aspirations, the last step to be taken is that of 'receiving'. Whenever you ask for something, you expect it to get delivered. This is what receiving is. In this step, you have to strengthen your chances of achieving your targets by taking actions and behaving as if you have created your desired reality. Expect the best coming to you. Live as if you are blessed by the energy of the universe. Visualisations are role-plays that you create in your mind with closed eyes. Receiving is a role-play that you engage in with open eyes. It is living in the future, but in the present moment.

Asking and believing is where you link your thoughts, beliefs, and feelings to your goals. Receiving helps in interlinking your actions to your goals. Since your subconscious mind is unable to differentiate between reality and imagination, it paves way for you to execute your imagination by guiding you in taking actions.

Positive AFFIRMATIONS for your goals

↓

Creative VISUALISATION of your goals

↓

Creation of OPPORTUNITIES

↓

You perform ACTIONS

↓

REALITY is created

Figure: Receiving is the last step in the process of fulfilment of your goals

Your goals will be fulfilled to the exact extent that you believed in receiving them. You have to act as if you are living in that future moment right now. It strengthens the chances of creating your desired reality. For example, if you dream of becoming a stand-up comedian, then stand up on some elevated platform assuming it to be your podium. Crack funny jokes in front of your imaginary audience. Shout out loud in joy for a houseful show. Imagine the audience's applause. Feel the pride and confidence you have in yourself. Such practices bring out the best in you because you become a proactive observer of the reality you want to create.

Approach towards Effective Receiving

The process of receiving will be completed when you start

behaving as if you are living the life of your dreams. You will be able to apply this step more easily after practising the approach explained in this chapter. It will help you enact your imagination well and assure victory. This will set a chain of events in motion, which will guide you towards your goal.

❖ Gratitude

The two most profound words that can put you in the state of receiving abundance in every phase of your life are 'Thank You'. There is nothing as great as saying thank you for what you have. In the words of spiritual teacher Brother David Steindl-Rast, "The root of joy is gratefulness . . . It is not joy that makes us grateful; it is gratitude that makes us joyful."

Be grateful for all that you have from the bottom of your heart. Being in the state of bliss after being thankful invites other positive feelings, people, and circumstances in your life, for which you can be thankful again. Gratitude gives you hope of receiving more fun-filled moments from the repository of the energy of the universe around you. Gratitude uplifts you by building your trust in your thought-power and the energy of the universe. When you are grateful for what you have at this moment, you attract other such moments in your life. Be thankful as if the things that you have written down in your goal list have been offered to you. In the words of Wallace D. Wattles, "Faith is born of gratitude. The grateful mind continually expects good things, and expectation becomes faith."

You can be thankful for so many things in your life—your family, house, money, education, food, health, kids, job, business, awards, talent, well-being, luxury, the sun, water, air, the nature around you, etc. The more thankful you are, the more reasons you will get to be thankful for. All aspects of your life will be enriched. Gratitude is like the accelerator of your car. Without it, it is almost impossible to reach the destination.

If you keep feeling sorry for yourself and are dissatisfied with your life, you will receive more disappointment. When you say, "Oh, I am such a loser with no luck!" your thoughts are pointed towards how vexed you are from your life. This makes you an observer who is creating a reality that contradicts his or her desires.

Some of you might be thinking that practising gratitude is not possible when you are living in a state of intense misery, like extreme poverty, being broke while having kids to feed, having no job, failure in exams, being in debt, suffering from a life-threatening disease, and whatnot! Well, here I can tell you that you can still be grateful for something. Maybe you could be thankful for being alive today, for trees that provide you oxygen, for your family, for having a roof above your head, for having a college degree, for having INR 100 in your pocket, or for having clothes on your body. Even when you feel that your existence is in turmoil, be thankful for the air you breathe because it gives you one more day to live and change your life!

Here, I am reminded of a beautiful experience shared by the bestselling author and spiritual teacher, Dr Joe Vitale, in one of his talks about gratitude. He recalled one occasion when he was broke, and at that time, he reluctantly decided to practise gratitude. He took a pencil and started feeling thankful for the usefulness of that pencil for writing so many things. This small act made him realise how important having a pencil is. His gratitude increased his energy. Then from one thank you to the other, he realised that he was thankful for so many things in his life. Starting from just a small piece of lead and wood, he drew to himself a life of prosperity and widespread reputation. This did not happen because of the pencil; it happened because of the feelings of thankfulness that he attached to it. Each day, if you start practising gratitude deliberately, you will identify many things that you can be thankful for.

Gratitude strengthens the bond between you and your goals. In essence, the emotions attached to this practise are vital for being a proactive thinker. This feeling of being grateful opens up doors for other beautiful feelings like happiness, pride, love, trust, serenity, hope, admiration, and enthusiasm. In 2013, psychologists Robert Emmons and Michael McCullough studied the effect of gratitude on the happiness and well-being of people. Their results showed that people who practised conscious savouring of positive situations regularly were more joyful and that they experienced a higher level of well-being than those who did not practise it. Therefore, start right now!

Conveying your gratitude on a daily basis is one of the best investments that you can make to transform your life. Count your blessings rather than sorrows. Appreciate the present for a better tomorrow. Each day, howsoever terrible it goes, will have at least one thing you could be grateful for. Before going to bed, after getting up in the morning, during meditation, or at any other time of the day, just acknowledge all that you have. Think of five people and five things that you are grateful for.

You can start by maintaining a daily gratitude journal. I call this gratitude journal my 'Blessings Book'. It gives me an opportunity to count and thank all that which I am blessed with. Once you start this habit of penning down your blessings, you will realise that life has so much to offer. At the end of each day, write about at least a few things that you were grateful for on that day. You can even write a detailed emotional paragraph on something in particular you are very grateful for.

When I left my job, I was reduced to a very limited social circle. My writing work and research kept me busy the entire day and I didn't get much time to socialise. During those days, without much adventure in my life, my Blessings Book consisted of some basic things that I was grateful for, like love, health, good food, etc. Then one day, I decided to dig deep into that day's proceedings to find other minor details that went well. To my astonishment, I identified so many other things that I could be grateful for—my spouse who came home early from work, my house-help, whose support meant so much while I was busy with writing, my evening walks in the neighbourhood, the beautiful plants in my balcony, the heavy rains that filled up the small pond in front of my house, and the panoramic view of the hills from the window beside my writing table. For so long, I remained ignorant of these beauties that life was offering me each day! In a day full of tasks and deadlines, cherishing small things in life can become a source of inspiration to move forward.

If you still feel that life has nothing good to offer you, just remember that there are millions of people out there who have lost their loved ones, who do not have anything to eat, who do not have a shade to cover their heads, who do not have enough money to send their children to school. Think of them and you may find something that you can be grateful for!

From now on, whenever you ask for some wish to be granted, first take a moment and acknowledge all those wishes that you have already been granted. Kabir, the 15th-century Indian mystic poet, captures the significance of paying gratitude very well in his couplet, "In anguish everyone prays to Him, in joy does none; To one who prays in happiness, how can sorrow come?"

❖ March towards Your Goals

Just as your thoughts should be synced with your goals, so should be your actions. When you think about achieving a particular goal, you have to do things that are in alignment with what you have asked for. Actions put you in the right energy zone. Thoughts bring your goals closer, and via actions, you receive them.

By being an action-oriented observer, you are signalling the energy of the universe, "Hey buddy, I am on the right track. So can you be a little fast in sending me my bundle of joy?" The most important part of receiving is to act as if you already have it. By taking the right actions, you are living as if you already are abundant, without any scarcity. So, go out and do something that makes you feel happier, richer, and healthier. In the next few sections, you will be further able to understand how you can create coherent actions and thoughts.

Your subconscious mind is a database of all that you have ever seen, heard, felt, or experienced—real or imaginary. When you start focusing on your aim, the brain sends you the most apt information in the form of memories, intuitions, ideas, plans, clues, sixth sense, etc. As you start creating the right opportunities, the mind opens up different ways to make you sense those opportunities. You have to identify these and walk forward. Taking action at this point is a vital step in the process of receiving. The role of the mind in initiating actions can be understood by the following examples:

- You are trying to qualify for the Cultural Student Exchange programme. Your mind provokes you to go to a seminar where you meet the president of the programme and he offers you some valuable tips on how to apply for the programme.
- You are looking forward to starting a trading firm, but you have no clue where to start. Your observation can create an opportunity where your mind urges you to read a business magazine that holds the key to kick-starting a budding trading firm.

Your affirmations and visualisations will cause opportunities to knock at your door. But what matters the most is that you identify them and take actions. Without action, your affirmations and visualisations will be like castles in the air. More often than not, your prayers will be answered; be ready to receive them with hands wide open. A solution will present itself if you are willing to cooperate. Nature opens up various doors for those who dare to explore its beauty. Global leadership expert, Robin Sharma, says it aptly, "Dream big. Start small. Act now."

The meditation sessions can also help you explore the actions you need to take. Here are a few questions that you can ask yourself during meditation:

- What would it take to achieve my targets?
- What can I do to open up new possibilities?

- What talent do I need to grow?
- What should be my next plan?
- How can I enhance my overall well-being?
- How should I plan my day to get more from it?
- What should I do for a healthy lifestyle?
- How can I become a calm and supportive partner?
- How can I improve upon my practice?
- How can I start my spiritual journey? and so on.

Dr Srini Pillay, assistant professor of psychiatry at Harvard Medical School and the author of *The Science Behind Law of Attraction*, brings to us another beautiful fact on how our intentions make us perform actions. He explains, "The brain regions involved in 'intention' are very connected to those regions involved in action. As a result, firing up those brain regions involved in intention will start to fire up your action centres. Intention needs to be strong enough for action to occur. Also, when you place your attention on a certain feeling (example, pain), it can worsen that feeling."

One thought will lead to the next, one skill will lead to the next, and one plan will lead to the next. Take the first action and execute the first plan. Do not wait because time will elapse rapidly and you will find that yet another day has passed leaving you in a miserable state. If you procrastinate today, you will never know how close you were to receiving. The Pareto Principle of 80-20 states that 20% of your effective actions lead to 80% of your success. So, begin now . . . right now!

To elaborate on the importance of taking actions, let me tell you about 'the butterfly effect'. This concept was popularised by meteorologist Edward N. Lorenz to understand weather forecast predictions. In popular culture, the butterfly effect is interpreted to mean that even a slightest event or action can have an immense impact on the outcome. Even the tiniest actions produce reverberations in the universal energy in one way or the other. Each outcome in your life is a result of the actions you have taken previously. Those little acts that you avoid today can inordinately delay your happiness.

Planning:

Imaginations turn into reality by acting upon them. Execution of actions often needs a plan. Plans should be time-based and concrete. This planning can be done by acquiring the right know-how, listening to your inner voice, success imaging, etc. All these aspects are discussed in the following pages. You can then see beyond the ordinary and act extraordinarily. Big goals can be broken down into smaller steps. You can make use of your happiness diary during this step as well. Dedicate one page for each goal and write bullet points stating time frames and actions you need to take. Every single day, try doing something that brings you closer to your goals. Even a small step that you take today will unfold the subsequent steps, and you will know what to do next.

You might encounter a few setbacks during this process, but small failures should not dishearten you. Things and situations that you consider as failures can actually be the most valuable turning points of your life. Do not be anxious to see the end. Take the first step—call your friend for the advice you need, tell your partner the things that have been hurting you in the relationship, ask your boss for the raise you deserve, head out to that showroom, visit some model houses, buy that magazine, join the club, connect with that online community, print pamphlets for your business, invite prospective clients to tea, publish that article, write that blog, post an online advertisement, register for that course, start your exercise regime, etc. Do whatever seems obvious and valuable.

Let us see this through some examples.

- If you want to sell your house, then go and look for a real estate agent, renovate your house so that it looks attractive to buyers, and keep networking about it in your circle so that the information may reach to some prospective buyer by word of mouth.
- If you want to get nominated for an award, then buy the dress you would wear on that big day, practise your winning speech confidently, behave like a winner, and experience the feelings that a winner would.

❖ Uplifting Your Environment

In this scenario, the term 'environment' means the surroundings in which you live, work, travel, or spend most of your time. It may be a little weird to consider that the receiving process can be affected by your environment, but from my personal experience, I have always found this practise to be fruitful. Let us see how.

Your environment is crucial in maintaining your high spirits. A beautiful, tidy, cosy, and decorated home is something you would always love to come back to. Your environment should reflect your goals. It should fill you with enthusiasm and spark. You should be able to feel the thrill of success when you are there. Clean and inspiring surroundings make you more joyful, passionate, and creative. It keeps you in a good mood and attracts more positive thoughts that result in a state of well-being. You become eager to take actions, do more, and recognise newer opportunities that were dormant earlier. Let me elaborate with some examples:

- If you have started a new business and haven't rented an office space yet, do not turn your entire house into a walking office by sitting here and there with your laptop and phone. Find a small corner in one of the rooms, set up your table, decorate the wall with a painting you would love to have in your office, and keep it tidy. Set your laptop and documents the way you would do in your office cabin. You can even buy a rolling executive chair to give you more feel. Whenever you are working, work from that space. Sitting in a lousy manner on your bed while talking to a client over the phone can decrease your enthusiasm and productivity.
- If you want to be a renowned guitarist, first find a special corner to keep your guitar and to play it. If you prefer sitting while playing, then find that perfect chair that is comfortable, and as you play, imagine a cheering audience in front of you.
- If you are an aspiring artist, arrange your best work systematically so that you can access it easily whenever you want. Go through it frequently and visualise the remarkable moment when your work will be displayed in an art gallery of your choice.
- If nature brings a smile on your face, place some plants in your balcony or create a backyard garden for yourself if you have the space. Sit there, enjoy the beauty, and pay gratitude for that moment.

Believe me, it will freshen you up after a tiring day and rejuvenate your mind with energetic thoughts.

These examples are just the tip of the iceberg. There is ample amount of creativity that you can bring in to change your environment to reflect your goals.

Dr Richard Wiseman, professor of public psychology at the University of Hertfordshire and a bestselling author, suggests that placing plants in the room fosters creativity. Also, if you are up for some creative task, decorate your room in green and avoid red, if possible. The role of a positive environment can be identified from the fact that the Chinese philosophical system has a whole metaphysical art based on it which is known as feng shui.

When I decided to write this book, I first bought a comfortable writing desk. Then, I stuck a large piece of thermocol (as a substitute for a pinboard) on the wall in front of me and pasted inspirational quotes and pictures on it. This was my vision board. On one side of the table were my favourite books, arranged in an orderly fashion, and on the other side was a small money plant pot and a beautiful pen stand. This was my version of a writer's desk. Whenever I sit there to write, I live a life of a successful writer. I love working in my decorated home office.

Sometimes it may be difficult to change things around you, but try and find that space for yourself as there can always be something that you can match with your goals. You can buy some related stuff, rearrange your home/ office, make things clean and tidy around you, decorate the space with some handcrafted work, change your neighbourhood, etc.

It is not always necessary to spend money to create a cordial environment. You can improvise and redesign or redecorate. I have done it for myself without spending unnecessary bucks on it. The most crucial thing to remember is that whatever you do, your surroundings should be clean. Cleanliness brings positive energy. It will help you meditate upon your goals more effectively. Marie Kondo, in her bestselling book, *The Life-Changing Magic of Tidying Up*, says, "A messy room equals a messy mind." And by now, I don't think that anyone of you wants a messy mind anymore!

If your life is filled with unanswered emails, unpaid bills, cluttered kitchen, dirty laundry, unfinished task, and messy wardrobes, you can never be in a pleasant mood for too long. Incomplete tasks keep reminding you about the mess you are in. The mess will affect you without you even realising this. For a good start, clean your mind, your house, and your tasks. This makes you more disciplined and strengthens your willpower. All this affects you in the long run.

❖ Success Imaging

The concept of success imaging is a real motivator. I came to know about it in an outstanding book, *Megaliving,* written by Robin Sharma. In simple terms, success imaging can be defined as becoming the mirror image of what or who you want to become. For example, if you want to be a world-famous tennis player, start doing what tennis champions do, read the books they read, practise the way they practise, read their articles and interviews, watch their matches, etc. This strengthens your belief and prepares you to receive the good fortune. When you do what a successful person or your idol would do, you are actually making your mind believe that you are as successful as them. As a result, all your thoughts and actions will be goal-oriented. Your actions will be perfect without any contradictions. The time lag between your observation and creation of reality will reduce.

In his book, *Think and Grow Rich*, Napoleon Hill, author of the first bestseller on the power of thoughts, calls this as the 'habit of hero-worship'. He explains that, long before writing the book, he entered into the habit of rebuilding himself by trying to imitate nine of his most admired men from history.

❖ Your Ultimate Aim—Happiness

Life should be an expression of joy and not a pursuit of joy. Happiness is to be found now, in the present moment. If you want to create a joyful life for yourself, you have to be happy right now. Happiness in the present can attract happiness in the future. What you give out will come back. Your happiness should not be governed by any ifs, buts, then, and now. While receiving, you cannot wait to be happy on some day in the future, as this reflects scarcity in the present.

The source of happiness lies within you. You are responsible for your happiness. If you believe that you will be happy if your spouse, friend, family, neighbour, client, or boss starts to do things in a certain way, then you are mistaken. How is this even possible? The journey is yours, the emotions are yours, the thoughts are yours, and the actions are yours . . . then how can your happiness depend on someone else? This understanding is absolutely essential if you want to move forward in this journey of self-improvement.

All emotions that make you feel happy will bring you closer to your goals. Happiness keeps you in alignment with your goals. The more you allow yourself to experience or imagine a joyful state of affairs, the more magnetic an observer you will become. Happiness is contagious as well. When you are happy, you will make people around you happy too. This, in turn, would result in an overall positive environment around you.

In his book *59 Seconds*, Professor Richard Wiseman talks about wonderful ways of being happy that I have shared here. One should buy experiences and not goods. A day well spent is often the day which has a good memory associated with it, such as a dinner with the family, adventure trekking, watching a good movie, vacationing, playing a sport, etc. Such experiences fill the soul with positive emotions that generate heartwarming memories. Do not be preoccupied with a materialistic lifestyle all the time. It can only provide you with short-term gratification. So, cook something new, go out, relax, sing, express gratitude, write in your happiness diary, watch comedy shows, walk in oneness with nature, dance, paint, listen to music, read a book, or do whatever makes you feel content from deep within. You can follow your hobbies. Hobbies make your creativity shine. They make you feel worthy and inspired.

Science has shown that acts of giving make us truly happy. Helping and being kind to any living being makes you feel happy in the long-term. Giving does not necessarily mean giving financial gifts. It can be a non-monetary help. I will discuss this in detail in subsequent sections. Lastly, a smiling face and demeanour of a happy person further enhance the chances of being happy.

❖ Appreciation vs Criticism

Appreciation is a freeway for the easy movement of positive energy. It brings a surge of positive emotions like joy and gratitude. Self-appreciation without false pride inspires you and elevates your thoughts to create more such qualities that can be appreciated. Appreciation of others for their character, help, talent, behaviour, or actions makes you feel good at heart and helps you evolve into a better person. Appreciation brings more smiles and laughter. It is rightly said, "What you appreciate, appreciates!" If you cannot appreciate something, how can you get it? Moreover, if you appreciate someone and are thankful for their presence in your life, you also get the credit of making someone smile.

Criticism, on the other hand, skews you from the path that you need to follow. It is a Pandora's box of troubles. When you criticise, you are either speaking ill of someone or something or are grumbling or quarrelling. All these strong negative words and emotions take you farther away from your goals by creating a contradictory reality in your mind. Instead of being judgemental, jealous, regretful, or angry, try being calm, compassionate, and humble. Resolve resentments and compliment and admire people. The Huna Philosophy says, "Bless that which you want."

❖ Intuition: Your Inner Guide

The time when I decided to quit my job and work towards my passion, I was looked at as someone with a 'messed-up life' by many people who knew me. (When you have a degree from IIT and you decide to quit your job in search of your passion, it is actually quite disorganised in the eyes of society we live in.) But my heart, my mind, and every cell in my body knew that I would never regret this period of my life. My inner voice stood by me all the time to give me the courage to do what I wanted to do rather than live a mediocre life and pretend to be happy. It made me believe that writing, for motivating people was my thing.

"Intuition is the ability to understand immediately without conscious reasoning and is sometimes explained as a 'gut feeling' about the rightness or wrongness of a person, place, situation, temporal episode, or object." (Simon M McCrea, 2010) Inner guidance or intuition does not involve the logic, equations, reasons, and statistics that you explore while surfing the Internet. It is the voice through which your soul talks to you when you sit with it in silence and believe in it. Intuition is the knowledge beyond what your five senses can perceive. Who exactly is sending you these hunches—maybe the brain or the subconscious mind or the consciousness or the energy of the universe—who knows? But one thing is for sure, it will come to you only in the direction in which your thought-process is aligned.

Research shows that intuition is not a superstitious phenomenon, as believed earlier. Intuition is a form of extrasensory perception (ESP). This faculty is available to everyone, albeit to varying degrees, like a skill. John Mihalasky, professor at New Jersey Institute of Technology and co-author of the book, *Executive ESP*, conducted a series of intuition tests and reported that executives with precognition abilities are better at making successful business decisions. In the words of Richard Branson, founder of Virgin Group, "I rely far more on gut instinct than researching huge amounts of statistics . . . We all have an intuitive sense of what's best—follow it!"

Research published by Soon et al. (2008) and Voss and Paller (2009) suggest that intuitive decisions are made ahead of time, by the subconscious mind, without our conscious awareness. The subconscious mind does so by decoding the pool of memories and information embedded into it or by tapping into the energy of the universe. You see, the whole thing is somewhere connected to your thoughts and beliefs. What you feed to your mind may result in an intuition later in life. Everything is linked to what you are thinking all the time.

Jack Canfield, co-author of the *Chicken Soup for The Soul* series, got the million-dollar idea of selling his book after he started engaging in the visualisation practise. His inner voice pointed the way towards an opportunity that changed his life forever.

Intuition can be in the form of vision (clairvoyance), hearing (clairaudience), or feeling (clairsentient). During receiving, awareness is important if you want to notice any subtle information. Being aware and conscious of self and surroundings prepare you to look through the snippets of information that you have been provided with. Sudden inspirations can come in the form of a signboard on the street, a magazine's cover page, a conference you attended, a dream, a flash of an idea, gut-feeling, etc.

The more you believe and practise this skill, the sooner you will master the act of getting guidance from your inner self. Meditation and visualisation are tools that can enhance your intuitive abilities. You can make a list of all sorts of intuitions that you keep receiving now and then. This will increase your trust in the process.

Using your inner voice as guidance can be very fruitful, especially when you start working on some new goals from your affirmation list. There will be times when you don't know where to start from or which direction to follow. When this happens, sit in silence, relax, and breathe deeply. Ask your inner self to throw some light on how to progress. You can ask for action steps, hints, information, ideas, opportunities, etc. Often, you will find answers to your problems during meditation, just before sleeping, or just before getting up from the bed in the morning.

If you want to gain detailed insights into the how and why of intuition, I suggest reading the works of Sonia Choquette, a celebrated author on intuition and visionary guidance. Also, on YouTube there is this wonderful guided meditation by Jason Marianoff which you can use to receive answers from your higher-self.

❖ Be a Giver

Adam M. Grant, professor at the University of Pennsylvania and author of the bestselling book, *Give and Take*, highlights the beauty of selfless giving in his book. According to his theory, those who lend their help to people without any motives of receiving return benefits are more successful in the longer run. The act of giving makes you joyous at heart, creating a feeling of contentment that elevates your thoughts and emotions.

The thought process at the time of giving is equally important. Some people give with an open heart (not necessarily money), radiating feelings of richness and contentment in their life. Others give with feelings of loss associated with what they give. Finally, there are those who have such a closed heart that they never wish to give anything to others. The last two groups exude the feeling of scarcity and lack and thus create more of it in their lives.

His Holiness the Dalai Lama beautifully mentions in his book, *Beyond Religion: Ethics for a Whole World*, "Giving material goods is one form of generosity, but one can extend an attitude of generosity into all one's behaviour. Being kind, attentive, and honest in dealing with others, offering praise where it is due, giving comfort and advise where they are needed, and simply sharing one's time with someone—all these are forms of generosity, and they do not require any particular level of material wealth."

When you become a free-giver, you build open doors for bountiful receiving. You portray to the energy of the universe that you have enough to share with others. Giving will multiply your happiness and you will lighten up someone else's life. It will make you and the world a kinder and joyous place to live in.

❖ Be Excited and Not Obsessed

A lengthy list of goals and action items might generate setbacks related to how and when they will be achieved. When you plant a seed, it is useless to fret about its growth every hour. Your work is to water it and provide it with sunlight. World-renowned advocate for alternative medicines and author, Deepak Chopra, highlights the importance of detachment from our desires. He elaborates, "In detachment lies the wisdom of uncertainty . . . in the wisdom of uncertainty lies the freedom from our past, from the known, which is the prison of past conditioning. And in our willingness to step into the unknown, the field of all possibilities, we surrender ourselves to the creative mind that orchestrates the dance of the universe."

Sometimes, you don't move closer to your aim even after practising correct belief systems, making affirmative wishes, and engaging in creative visualisation. It is of considerable value to understand that when you are observing and trying to receive, your goals should be positive desires and not desperate demands. If you are obsessed about the completion of your goal or you want it too badly, it reflects the scarcity of these desires in the present moment. Your feelings and thoughts of scarcity will unknowingly produce unconscious beliefs of lack. If you are obsessed and desperate, your emotions are negative and the energy around you is negative. It is not sufficient to have specific thoughts; the emotions enveloping the thoughts are equally important.

Your goals are not fulfilled by doing the ABR process over and over again for the same goal. You have to stop at one point. You have to do your part and then walk out in expectation of receiving the best outcome. If you will keep whirling in the cycle of affirmation and visualisation, you will signal that your desire is still unfulfilled. You will get caught up in a mesh. Your efforts should be smooth and gentle in the process of creation. If you have followed the Ask-Believe-Receive process sincerely, your efforts will bear fruit. Separating oneself from the anxiousness of the outcome won't be difficult for such an observer. If you have planted positive thoughts in your mind and taken required actions, then something wonderful will pop out from it. You should respect the time lag instead of fretting about it. Your anxiousness may drop you one level below on the positivity scale, thus delaying the outcome.

I cannot emphasise enough that 'letting go' is one of the very important tools required for manifestation. If you have played your part well, then you will have a certain sense of surety and satisfaction in the fulfilment of your wishes. There will be tranquillity and a sense of knowing. This feeling is important as it highlights that you have surpassed the reality inertia and have been a good observer with efficacious subconscious beliefs. Only then, you start resonating with your goal and become one with it in the present moment.

When thoughts of anxiousness and doubts arise, close your eyes and de-stress. Breathe in a rhythmic pattern (5-5-2) with a smiling face. Keep calm and remember the fact that your mind and the energy of the universe are at work. If you have been a powerful observer, then you have done your part. Now, just share the rest of the responsibility of the creation process with the energy of the universe around you. Do what is within your reach and then let go of any scepticism. Have faith. You do not have to see the whole staircase at the beginning. Climb one step at a time and see your mini-goals unfolding in each step. Don't cling so badly to your desires that it keeps you from changing them into reality. The act of letting go reflects your faith in thought-power, the mind, and the creation process. It is the final cord of connection between your goals and their accomplishment.

Further, for the fulfilment of your goals, don't force the process of creation to follow the only path that you know. Your goals can be achieved through many other unknown ways that you haven't even thought of. Maybe you are served in a better way than you choose to receive! Do not restrict yourself. At one point, you have to pull back and let the higher power bring something rewarding for you. If you have asked and believed in a conscious way, better opportunities will line up at your doorstep.

Also, the time lag between a desire and its fulfilment is worthy in itself. It prepares you to fully understand the consequences of the intention so that there are no regrets later in life. So, do not be impatient.

❖ Handling Sceptics and Pessimists

You are trying to break the age-old method of human thinking; so, you are surely going to attract some frowns. In Chapter 2, we discussed more about the prevailing scepticism around the concept of the thought-power. Since you have reached this point in the book, it clearly shows that you are very fascinated about this new knowledge and have started your journey towards engaging in proactive thinking by practising the various methods listed in the book. But your life is not just limited to you; you have your friends, partner, spouse, parents, colleagues, and others who find this very idea too good to be true. If you do not act mature enough, this mismatch of ideas between you and those around you can end up in a bad note in two ways.

First, maybe the people around you are in the negative energy zone. They do not know what they are capable of achieving and how powerful their thoughts are. So, if you try to impose yourself on them, you may be mocked at for believing in some New Age mumbo jumbo.

Second, you may be asked to live in the real and practical world that is actually made up of pain and challenges—as this is a general reality for many. You may be made to think that, in real life, your thoughts do not decide your fate, but rather your family, society, and the government do.

Try to understand that each one's mindset is different and forcing yourself on someone is going to lead into steamy discussions and conflicts, leaving both of you in a negative energy zone. It may be difficult for some of your loved ones to change their beliefs and accept an out-of-the-box concept. But that's okay. You are responsible for your thoughts and not for what others think. Now, when you know the whole truth behind thought-power, you cannot afford to lower your positive energy. If you do not want their pessimistic approach to harm you or influence you, work on your positive emotions. No one is allowed to play with your mood until you allow them to. Your world is ruled inside out and not the other way round.

The sceptics around you are not to be mistaken for their different opinion. They are telling you what they have been told since childhood. They are preaching what they know and believe in. You just focus on practising what you know and believe in.

I suggest that you continue practising the ABR process with dedication. All those who try to make a dent in the universe are opposed at first. Create your dream life one step at a time. Do not preach others on thought-power. Let your work speak. Attract good things towards yourself and think about having good times with those around you. When the change you keep speaking about becomes true, you will be able to inspire others to believe in themselves and in the thought-power. I have witnessed it for myself that good habits are infectious. If you are inspired and are following a good ritual then you will surely create a positive impact on people around you. Give yourself a chance, and, for once, ignore all the negativity which others convey.

❖ Taking Care of Your Health

A healthy body will have a healthy mind and a healthy mind will have healthy thoughts. So, take care of your health on a daily basis. Exercise and a wholesome diet are essential for keeping your body healthy. Exercise not only tones your muscles but also conditions your mind to be more focused and stable. Such a mind will be easy to control. You will find that your stamina and energy will increase day-by-day as you put yourself on some kind of exercise regime. It can be brisk walking, running, yoga, aerobics, dance, etc.

Similarly, eat a well-planned nutritious diet. Your brain consumes the most energy as compared to any other part of your body. So, feed it right. Consider it this way; when you are famished, you get irritated easily and are unable to focus on a tough task. So, keep your brain packed with energy so that it can focus more on creating the right thoughts. Not just your thoughts, your actions will also improve when you are eating healthy. You will be fully charged to take the risk, dream big, do more, and reach your peak potential. The great Buddha once said, "To keep the body in good health is a duty, otherwise we shall not be able to keep our mind strong and clear."

It is in your hand to achieve mental poise. Good health is the best gift you can offer to your brain which is the inception of your thinking. If you want to become a proactive thinker, you have to take control of what you are thinking and for this, you have to ensure that your mind and body are in the best state.

❖ Acknowledge Small Wins

As you begin this new journey towards self-transformation, it is important to acknowledge the efforts you make during your progress. Each good thought, each effort to control your anger, each time you express gratitude, each time you complete a visualisation session, etc.—all of these are reasons to praise yourself. Celebrating small wins keeps you motivated. It gives a feeling of satisfaction that you are never alone on this journey. It removes doubts and inspires you to do more.

One way to acknowledge these wins is by jotting them down in your happiness diary. All the signs, proofs, incidents, habits, actions, synchronicities, and intuitions that thought-power brings towards you are different forms of your growth. In a while, you can also treat yourself with ice cream or a movie or an extra hour of sleep! These small doses of motivation make the journey even more worth travelling.

Summary

"Change is the end result of all true learnings."
—Leo Buscaglia (author)

The reality that life is under your control gives so much relief. But at the same time, it comes with the responsibility of making your life a pleasant gift.

The first step in the process of change is 'awareness'. No change is ever possible without awareness. Now, that you are aware that the key to a happy life lies within you, make intelligent choices of your thoughts. Embark upon a path of self-improvement by utilising the knowledge you have absorbed.

Your Life = f (your mindset, beliefs, goals, actions, asking, believing, receiving)

ACKNOWLEDGEMENTS

In the entire process of sharing this wonderful information with my readers, there have been many people who stood by me and believed in me.

I am grateful to the universe for giving me the courage to uncover a totally different phase of my life and excel in it. I am grateful to all the motivational authors and coaches who are spreading this magnificent knowledge around them and inspiring people.

I am grateful to my husband, Abhinav Nigam, for his immense love and care. The emotional, physical, and financial support that he has provided me during this time is unparalleled. It was because of him I could take the courageous decision of leaving my job and follow my life's purpose and passion. He has always been there to patiently listen to my thoughts and advise me throughout my life, especially while I was writing this book. His worldly wisdom and simple living have evolved me into a better person. I am grateful to my little angel Prisha for being a fountain of happiness and motivation in my life and for teaching me forbearance. She inspires me to do great things in life and leave a wonderful legacy behind.

I am grateful to my father, Devendra Nath Srivastava, for his unconditional love and belief in my talents. He has always encouraged me to aspire for greatness in life. His sacrifices helped me in becoming self-reliant. It was because of him that I was raised in a home with a library, which started my journey into the world of books. I am grateful to my mother, Manju Devendra, for her affectionate nurturing. She has been a support pillar during all the trials of life and has always motivated me to be an independent woman. I am grateful to my brother, Aakash Srivastava, for strongly supporting me in this decision of sharing my knowledge through this book. I am thankful to him and Murtaza Salumber for launching my online platform—authorswati.com.

I am grateful to my father-in-law, Priya Vivek Nigam and mother-in-law, Manjula Nigam, for their never-ending support and affection. I am thankful to Ankuri, my sister-in-law, for her guidance on various book marketing perspectives.

I am grateful to my publisher, Hay House India, for believing in my work and offering me this wonderful opportunity to publish my work. I am obliged to Raghav Khattar for helping me in the submission of my manuscript and resolving my queries throughout this process. I am immensely thankful to my editor, Aditya Jarial, for bringing the manuscript into its best form. I am also thankful to Sonali Pawar and Nupur Hirani for their contributions towards the book finalisation and marketing.

I am grateful to all my relatives, friends, and teachers who have supported me in different endeavours of my life. I would also like to mention here a few names that have played a huge role in shaping my personality and developing my interest in reading and writing. My teachers from my school, Dr V.S.E.C—Jyotsana Pandey, Mrs Suman, Shruti Mishra, Neelima Raizada, and Vikas Saxena. My teachers from Amity University—Dr Rachna Singh, Dr Sayali Mukherjee, and Dr Nalina Singh and my cousin, Jyoti Srivastava. I am also indebted to three wonderful mentors in my life who believed in my talent and gave me the confidence in my abilities—Dr Jonaki Sen (IIT Kanpur), Dr Arun Kumar (IIT Delhi), and Dr Vishnu Ranade (General Electric, GE).

With Love & Gratitude,
Swati Srivastava

About the Author

Swati Srivastava is an engineer turned writer. After graduating from IIT Delhi, she worked at General Electric (GE). She first came to know about the powers of the human mind through Robin Sharma's book *MegaLiving* in 2012. Since then, through her efforts and by consciously applying thought-power in her life, she kept on adding one star after another to her life—from a prestigious college to a reputed job and then a wonderful life partner and an angel baby girl.

With time, she realised that there is something more to her existence as thought-provoking questions started hitting her. With a lot of thinking and even a lot more courage, she quit her MNC job in pursuit of the real purpose of her life.

Soon, she switched to her ultimate calling and moved away from all other career options. She clubbed her love for inspirational literature and writing to become a motivational writer. The journey had many trials but today, she is proud of listening to her inner voice and rising above the fear of "What will people say?" The confidence and belief in the power of her thoughts helped her find her purpose, passion, and contentment in life.

Through her writings, she wants to convey to people at large, the importance of our thoughts, the role of beliefs in

. . . *continued*

shaping our destiny, and success tools for having thoughts that converge to create a reality out of our wish list.

- ❖ Subscribe for author's blogs, bonus offers and book updates at authorswati.com
- ❖ Connect with the author on social media:
    - Facebook: @swatisrivastava.author
    - Instagram: @swatisrivastava.author
- ❖ You can send your feedback at feedback@authorswati.com
- ❖ For any other queries, you can write to the author at contact@authorswati.com